ROBERT WYETH

PREHISTORIC MEN WERE SAVAGES?

WORKBOOK PRESS LLC
187 E Warm Springs Rd,
Suite B285, Las Vegas, NV 89119, USA

Website: https://workbookpress.com/
Hotline: 1-888-818-4856
Email: admin@workbookpress.com

Ordering Information:
Quantity sales. Special discounts are available on quantity purchases by corporations, associations, and others.
For details, contact the publisher at the address above.

Library of Congress Control Number:

ISBN-13:   978-1-960752-03-1 (Paperback Version)
              978-1-960752-02-4 (Digital Version)

REV. DATE: 09/21/2022

Prehistoric Men Were Savages?

Robert Wyeth

Contents

Acknowledgements

Most of the verses were taken from the NIV Bible:

The Holy Bible, New International Version ®, copyright 1973, 1978, 1984 by International Bible Society.

Copyright 1985 by the Zondervan Corporation.

Anglicisation 1987 by the Hodder and Stoughton Limited.

This edition first presented in Great Britain in 1987.

Other versions:

Holy Bible, New Living Translation ®, copyright 1996, 2004 by Tyndale Charitable Trust, issued by the Tyndale House Publishers.

The Holy Bible containing the Old and New Testaments the New King James Version. Copyright 1979, 1980 by Thomas Nelson Inc. Published by Broadman & Holman Publishers, Nashville. Tennessee.

It contains the 1611 version of the Authorised Version for the Holy Scriptures.

Summary

Looking through the Bible, men were immensely powerful in thought, emotions, goals, practice and even skilled. They did more things than we could do today, even with our technology and computing machines.

When the flood came, the whole record of what they were doing was lost and gone, but the stones still remained lodged in the ground. We can see over many countries what insight and practice, butting up all sorts of shapes and sizes with the weight of hundreds of tons locking together. This is why we know that in the past they were indeed clever and had enormous power. Whether it was steam, mechanical or other suitable things we cannot be sure.

One thing that God has as its creation and the other is what men were thinking, all based on what the Bible teaches. There is no evidence that in the beginning when God created man he was supremely fit and agile. Over the years, men and women deteriorated from what they had been doing. God's curse would come true (see Genesis ch.3 v16-19).

It is laughable with the false teaching and false prophets, with books, writings and education. Men insisted that they came down from trees or came up out of the water. They would demand that the world was billions of years old from all the rocks. That animals were evolving to make one kind be another kind. It is false practice; no-one was there in the beginning, so no-one could say, 'It was like that'.

They failed to take into account what the Bible counsels or directs that in the beginning God created man. That he sinned and thought he could do better than God. Even professors and eminent teachers would dismiss that as nonsense. The study of the Bible is the key to hold on to and this cuts across the whole purpose and imagined thinking that others believe. Go out when it is dark, look up at the sky and count the number of stars. Which one is the farthest away from you?

God counts the stars and each has its name (see Psalm ch.147 v4). Man is weak and helpless, but God is strong and mighty. So who do you pick?

A Young Earth

Some Equations

There's two equations that we an use to work out the force of the earth and the internal energy. How young is the whole solar system?

For example:

The first law came in 1850 from Rudolf Clausius and from William Rankine. The First Law of Thermodynamics distinguishes heat, work and matter transfers, is $U = Q - W$.

U, change in internal energy.

Q, heat added.

W, work done by the system.

This is the law of conservation of energy, adapted for thermodynamic processes, like heat or work done on a system. The law of conservation of energy states that the total energy of an isolated system is constant, energy cannot be transformed from one form to another; neither created or destroyed by the process.

- - - - - - -

The second law when Isaac Newton published in 1687 then Newton used them to explain and investigate the motion of many physical objects and systems. Newton's Second Law, a body remains at rest or in motion or at a constant speed in a straight line, unless acted upon by a force.

Describes a simple relationship between the acceleration of an object with mass and net force acting on that object, is $F = ma$.

F, force.

m, mass.

a, acceleration.

These are the two laws which describe the earth and its moon, rotating around the sun. It is true for the whole cosmos of the solar system.

Comets

Comets are small low density mass that orbits the sun and other stars that shine brightly we can see them in the sky. A comet is very small, ranging from 1 or 30 miles in overall diameter.

As they come near the sun, some of their icy material is vaporised presenting a tail that forms away from the sun when it is hot. It sweeps behind the comet by its interaction with the solar wind when it passes around the sun. The comets are tiny and are only visible from within the earth.

The presence of tails tells us that the comet are continually losing mass. It is true that comets are only temporary. If the solar system were 4.6 billion years old (as some men think) all of our complete system of comets should have been exhausted long ago. But we still see them.

Moon

Ever since telescopes were invented, observers have been reporting many colour changes. Bright and coloured spots appear and streaks, clouds, hazes and veils on the moon. Since these are short lived, they are called Transient Lunar Phenomena and they refer to the geological presence of the moon.

Since the moon is about one fourth of the size of the earth, heavy masses would fall to the centre and the moon would cool much faster than the earth. But it is not so. The moon is still have is very much alive and billion years that men have accounted for, would see none of the colour changes. It would be flat and stable.

Jupiter and Neptune

Jupiter and Neptune actually radiates nearly twice as much power as it receives from the sun, but mostly it is infrared. The usual explanation is that the two giants are shrinking. This converts gravitational energy into internal heat under the law of conservation energy. But it is totally unproven.

The average temperature in Jupiter's upper atmosphere is 426 degrees Centigrade, almost as hot as the surface of Venus. This causes an 'energy crises'. A new study has found that the planets strong magnetic field is contributing the problem, but what about Neptune a distance much farther away?

Others have said that nuclear reactions as a result of burning heavy hydrogen on Jupiter. But this is not clear for Neptune, it is three billion miles away from the sun. Neptune is still very cold, usually around minus 214 degrees Centigrade.

Since they are massive and they have not had the time to cool down, which means that the billion years is not possible at all. This proposal is dismissive, why are the two giants radiating infrared heat? What causes it? We don't know.

Big Bang

Most recent books contains the 'big bang' where the earth started with an explosion and then carried on expanding outwards. It will be hot like in a furnace where metal is formed back to fluids. We can pour it out like water flowing from the furnace.

Now the earth was formless and empty, darkness was over the surface of the deep, and the Spirit of God was hovering over the waters Genesis ch.1 v2

In the beginning, the earth was very cold and covered with water. God was there but man was not even present back then.

If the world was covered with water, the whole purpose of the 'big bang' is meaningless and is not basically true. The whole purpose of the world starts with the earth and then after that we see the sun and stars forming.

It is a separate act of God out of nothing.

- - - - - - -

So who do you trust, God or man? The Scriptures or man's thought? God created the earth, but man in his intelligence and all his equipment and computers has forgotten and silenced God speaking through the Bible.

The fool says in his heart, "There is no God."… All have turned aside, they have together become corrupt; there is no one who does good, not even one. Psalm ch.14 v1, v3

We see man who is corrupt and cannot see God in his wisdom who created everything, even the stars, the mountains, the rivers, the animals and even man.

The sinful mind is hostile to God. It does not submit to God's law, nor can it do so. Romans ch.8 v7.

Man is blind or irresponsible. For God's laws came to pass and the books of the Bible was written down many years ago. We see the sinful mind is hostile, opposed to God. Many minds think over the years and we have another plan the 'big bang' which is taught through education, contradicting God in his wonderful creation.

Solar System

We can see here on earth any galaxy, particularly if we have a binoculars or a telescope and it is a clear night. A galaxy is a countless number of stars and some, if not all, would be located in a barred spiral, like the Milky Way our own galaxy.

The outside stars are slower than the inside stars and it is assumed they are rotating around a black hole. The ones in the middle have a shorter time and those in the outside have a longer time. This means the stars in the outside are travelling faster than the stars in the middle.

If the earth was billions of years old then the outside stars will contract and slow and be the same as the inside stars. The galaxy would reduce in size and the spirals would move closer to a circle, because the stars would slow down and the gravity of the galaxy would affect them.

We can see that it is the same size here on earth. Therefore, the solar system is not that old.

- - - - - - -

A star uses up its gases in the nuclear reactions taking place at its core. The star is starting to die. Like the sun it gradually sheds material from its outer layers. Stars end its life in a gigantic explosion called a supernova because the explosion looks like a bright new star. Or, the star uses up the hydrogen and he surface cools and reddens.

We understand that when mankind sinned and went to the tree of the knowledge of good and evil (see Genesis ch.2 v18) and took the fruit and ate it (see Genesis ch.3 v6), they sinned against God.

The Lord cursed all of the trees, animals, mankind and even stars came to their end of their life, they would have to die. It wasn't that way when God created everything. He made everything 'good'.

Carbon Atoms

Carbon is chemical element with the symbol, C and atomic number 6. Making four covalent chemical bonds, it belongs to group 14 of the Periodic Table. It is the hardest material known to man, more or less inert, able to withstand the strongest and most corrosive of acids.

Carbon 12 and Carbon 14 are two isotopes of the element carbon. The difference is the number of neutrons in each of their atoms. Carbon 12 and Carbon 13 are stable, but Carbon 14 is unstable. Carbon 14 has to many neutrons to be stable.

To achieve stability, the atom must make adjustments, the end result is a stable atom. This process of changing one element into another element is called radioactive decay, or radiometric dating.

It is complicated, but it is necessary to see how the rocks are consisting off, or coming to their 'rock date' when they were made.

Dating Rocks

The method for Carbon 14 is not used to date rocks, because most rocks do not contain carbon. We must find rocks that have the isotopes in minute quantities and then we can date them.

Because the short life of Carbon 14 it has a half-life of 5,730 years and after that the spare neutron should have decayed into nitrogen. Nitrogen is a colourless, odourless gas that is the most plentiful in Earth's atmosphere and is a constituent of all living matter.

But there are some rock we can date. Carbon dating is only accurate for dating rocks up to tens of thousand of years old because of the half-life. Most rocks are much older than this, therefore geologists must therefore find and use elements with longer half-lives like uranium and argon.

The method of using Carbon 14 to date rocks is only allowable for up to 5,730 years old. If you want to do this, you have to select another element. Most geologists do not use all four main radioactive clocks to date a rock unit, this is considered a waste of time and money. Sometimes, though using different parent radioisotopes to date a rock unit, but they all have different dates.

So how do we know the date of rocks?

Carbon 14

This method, Carbon 14 was developed by the American physicist William F Libby in 1946. His reasoning was based on a belief in evolution which assumes the world must be billions of years old. He noted that the atmosphere did not appear to be stable or equilibrium; he just ignored it and assumed that it would go away. But it didn't.

To do any radiometric dating the assumption was:

> Any ideal, initial amounts?

> Was any amount added?

> Was any amount removed?

> Has the rate of decay altered?

But the ratio of Carbon 14 to Carbon 12 is not constant at all:

> The influx of salts into the oceans.

> The rate of decay of the earth's magnetic field.

> The growth rate of the human population.

> The Genesis flood buried large amount of carbon.

Why? Each of the radioactive clocks must have decayed at different ages, faster rates in the past, or the ratio is not constant at all.

This seems pointless to work out the date of a rock item using Carbon 14. Why do they do it? It seems pointless to work out the date of a rock that is more than 5,700 years old. Because it is cheap, ignores the assumptions above and is not constant at all.

Most rocks are dated by Carbon 14 and gives rise to a weird dating system, including billions of years old.

Biblical Information

In the beginning God created the heavens and the earth. Genesis ch.1 v1

He created the all of the solar system out of nothing. But the Bible starts with God, he is not explained, he is just there. Who created God? We don't know, we are not expected to learn, we just have to acknowledge in his superior intellect and wisdom.

God's invisible qualities – his eternal power and divine nature – have been clearly seen, being understood for what he has made, so that men are without excuse. Romans ch.1 v20

However, we know what he has achieved, the creation around us. The mountains, the rivers and the land where we live. The animals, the birds and the fish he created all of that. We understand the sun, the moon and the stars which gives us our seasons. Men are expected to realise that God made everything, and there is no excuse to say, 'We don't know'. We definitely should know.

God said, "As long as the earth endures, seedtime and harvest, cold and heat, summer and winter, day and night will never cease." Genesis ch.8 v22

We know that the earth revolves around the sun. The day and night which rotates around the earth's axis. The axis is off-set which gives us summer and winter. This is what God has decided for us. He will set it in motion for as long as he decided; it will not cease to be present. Whatever mankind can do.

This is what the Scripture tells us, it starts with Israel and goes on to explain why Jesus had to die. This is the whole truth of God and he has explained it to us in the Bible and we are expect to read and study it.

When Did Men Appear?

We start with dating information in the Bible, you just have to know where to look. So when did mankind appear?

*When Adam had lived **130** years he had a son in his own likeness, in his own image, and he named him Seth. Genesis ch.5 v3*

Seth he lived 105 years he became the father of

> Enosh he lived 90 years and had,
>
> Kenan he lived 70 years and had,
>
> Mahalalal he lived 65 years and had,
>
> Jared he lived 162 years and had,
>
> Enoch he lived 65 years and had,
>
> Methuselah he loved 187 year and had,
>
> Lamech he lived 182 years and had Noah.
>
> Noah he lived 500 years and had Shem, Ham and Japheth.

Its a total of **1426** years from Seth to Noah (see Genesis ch.5 v3-32).

Shem was 100 years old he became the father of

> Arphaxad he lived 35 years and had,
>
> Shelah he lived 30 years and had,
>
> Eber he lived 34 years and had,
>
> Peleg he lived 30 years and had,
>
> Reu he lived 32 years and had,
>
> Sarug he lived 30 years and had,
>
> Nahor he lived 29 years and had,

Terah he lived 70 year and had,

Abraham he lived 86 years.

It is a total of **390** years form Shem to Abraham (see Genesis ch.11 v10-32).

This there were fourteen generations in all from Abraham to David, fourteen from David to the exile in Babylon, and fourteen from the exile to the Christ. Mathew ch.1 v17.

This is a total of 42 generations from Abraham to Jesus, say about each of 50 years gives us **2100** years.

From Jesus to us we will have **2200** years up to date.

It gives a total of men added up to 130 + 1426 + 390 + 2100 + 2200 = **6246 years**.

Whether the believers or otherwise, most scholars would agree that Abraham lived about 2000 BC. This is done with the Hebrew Masoretic text which is what most English translations are based upon. Two of the most popular are the work done Archbishop James Usher AD 1581-1656 and later by Dr. Floyd Jones. It was work done by both of them was 4004 BC, before Jesus Christ.

The age of the world was 5 days previously, so the world was begun in **6251 years**.

Prior to the AD 1700, few believed in an old earth dating back millions of years. The approximate age of the earth was **6000 years** old, but the recent was only challenged in the 18th century for the work done by radiation on the rocks, using Carbon 14 which is wildly inaccurate and false.

Adoption

The process of all kinds of animals to change one into another. This is a man-made choice to work out how the animals, bird and fish started out. It is a figment of the imagination because the world didn't begin until a few thousand years ago.

God said, "Let the water teem with living creatures, and let birds fly above the earth across the expanse of the sky ... according to their kinds, and every winged bird according to its kind." Genesis ch.1 v20

God said, "Let the land produce living creatures according to their kinds ... God made the wild animals according to their kinds, the livestock according to their kinds, and all the creatures that move along the ground according to their kinds." Genesis ch.1 v24-25

In the ark when God wiped out the rest of all creation:

You to bring into the ark two out of all the living creatures, male and female, to keep them alive with you. Two of every kind of bird, of every kind of animal and every kind of creature that moves along the ground will come to you to be kept alive. Genesis ch.6 v19-20

God didn't have baby birds and animals, he created them as mature kinds. From the start of creation to the flood every living thing, male and female of the kind were there in the beginning. Living things, like:

Kingdom - it is the largest group.

Phylum - the main division of an animal.

Class - rank of order of things.

Order - is a part of a class.

Family - a large collection of species.

Genus - a small collection similar species.

Species - sub-divided up, like we have a 'tiger'.

This is how we work out the kind of animals and birds. Each had a separate identity, or a kind. There's no evidence that two of each kind might cross over to another as part of an adoption. Consisting of the work they carry out.

How birds and animals work:

Reproduction rates - a fly up to 900 per year to a crocodile 50 per year.

Speeds - ostrich 45 mph to a cheetah 60 mph.

lifespan - fox 8 years to an elephant 70 years.

Temperatures - salmon 20 degrees C to a lizard 18 degree C.

Gestation period - whale 480 days to a mouse 20 days.

Heart rates - seal 10 beats/min to an hummingbird 1,200 beats/min.

Energy needs - robin 90 kJ to a giraffe 152,000 kJ.

Hearing ranges - dog 10-35,000 in Hz to a frog 100-2,500 Hz

Sleep requirements - sloth 20 sleeps/day to a squirrel 14 sleeps/day

There is no way any kind of animal from its kind can work with another kind of animal. All have the same category or character. God made each of us as its kind. There's no difference and no separation. Each one was totally unique.

Dinosaur Dating

Fossils themselves and the sedimentary rocks they are found in are very difficult to date directly. Instead, other methods are used to work our a fossil's age. These include radiometric dating of the volcanic layers above or below the fossils or by comparisons to similar rocks and fossils of known ages.

After extensive testing over many years, it was concluded that Uranium-Helium dating is highly unreliable because the small helium atom diffuses easily out of minerals over geologic time. As a result this method is not used except in rare and highly specialised applications.

All living things take in carbon from eating to breathing. When a bird or animal dies the amount of carbon will decrease or become less and less. The smaller the ratio, the longer the bird or animal has been dead. But the half-life of Carbon 14 expires in 5,730 years as we have already seen.

So man-made explanations for the date of dinosaurs under Carbon 14 giving billions of years old are false and inaccurate. They must have been when God created the birds and animals.

The Universe

We assume that God is like us, but he is not. He is more powerful and strong than we could even imagine.

Hubble a telescope above us out in space has revealed an estimated 100 billion galaxies, but the number is more than that even 200 billion galaxies.

The deeper we look into space the more galaxies we find. We understand that a lightyear (ly) is the distance light travel in one year, but at the speed of light. This is due to 9.46 million km / 5.88 million miles. Less than 10 stars are within 10 ly.

The Milky Way galaxy is about 100,000 ly across and is made up of billion of stars. On average the stars are 4 ly apart. The radius across the universe is believed to be 15 billion ly away.

The Lord merely spoke, and the heavens were created. He breathed the word, and all the stars were born. Psalm ch.33 v6 (NLT)

He determines the number of the stars and calls them each by name. Psalm ch.147 v4

We can't even count the number of stars, but God has a record of each and he calls them by name. He knows what the stars are doing, he goes there and sees what they are doing. How could he speak and the stars began? He made it so, we don't find baby stars, they each have a purpose to which God has designed and created.

We fail to work out the measurement of one galaxy with all our computers to map the distance, subject and objective of each star. What about the stars behind each other? Stars that we can't see from earth?

What Were They Doing?

Archery

Archery is a person who shoots with a bow and arrow.

The flood would have wiped out all the mechanisms to make a bow before that and the flood lasted 150 days and covered everything (see Genesis ch.7 v22-24). In the ark, there were no weapons that could be used so the people had to make it again. It is enough time to make a bow and arrows without any engineering means.

Sometimes the bow had a single curve or a double curve and it was made of seasoned wood. The bow-string was commonly ox-gut and the arrows were made of reed or light wood tipped with metal. To string them the lower end was held down with the foot, while the upper end was bent down to fasten the string in a notch. This explains the Hebrew word 'to tread the bow' which means 'to string it'.

- - - - - - -

God was with the boy as he grew up. He lived in the desert and became an archer. Genesis ch.21 v20

Sarah was barren and she had no children (see Genesis ch.11 v30). But Abraham had a son with Hagar the Egyptian, while Abraham was in Canaan. The baby was called Ishmael and Abraham was eighty six years old (see Genesis ch.16 v15-16). Hagar ran away from her mistress because she had a boy and Sarah didn't. Then Sarah had a boy called Isaac.

She said to Abraham, "Get rid of that slave woman and her son, for that slave woman's son will never share in the inheritance with my son Isaac." Genesis ch.21 v10

This was a turning moment for Ishmael, for God led him into the desert of Beersheba to be a great nation, he became an archer (see Genesis ch.21 v18; ch.25 v18). There was deep hostility between the brothers over Ishmael being rejected from his home.

- - - - - - -

Issac said, "I am now an old man and don't know the day of my death. Now then, get your weapons - your quiver and bow - and go out to the open country to hunt some wild game for me. Genesis ch.27 v3

Esau became a skilful hunter looking for wild game to bring to his family. He was out in the open country in Canaan with the trees and rivers (see Genesis ch.25 v27). He was out more than he was at home. He was partial to wild game like antelope and deer.

The most noticeable difference is the antelope they have two horns that deer do not have. They live in the wild shrub lands of Palestine. They eat grass, leaves and shoots of trees. Most deer live in herds and under attack the deer flees away.

Esau would know that, but he was out in the open country and he set himself to wait and watch. For he was a good hunter, his clothes were torn from what he had been doing and smelt of the open range. He had good eyesight and worked out that he would be downwind to get his smell away the animals. There is a river running through Beersheba going out to the Mediterranean Sea, so the animals would come to drink. Even Esau could bring down a deer while he was hiding in the grass.

- - - - - - -

And to you, as one who is over your brothers, I give the ridge of land. I took from the Amorites with my sword and bow. Genesis ch.48 v22

There are two sort of weapons used, the bow is used for distance and the sword is used hand-to-hand fighting. Jacob when he was old, explained to Joseph that he overcame the Amorites on the ridge of land. He must have had help from his many sons. He gave it to Joseph later because he was the favourite son. He didn't learn from his sons what they did to Joseph by overpowering him to take him away as a slave. He made Joseph wear a brightly coloured coat that marked him out as special to him, but his brothers could not say a kind word to him (see Genesis ch.37 v3-4).

The Ammorites kingdom was located between Moab and Edom, near the northern end of the Dead Sea. The Israelites must have gone through the Amorites for the plains of Moab, to go over the River Jordan to Jericho. There was only a ford to pass the River Jordan which passes through the hills (see Joshua ch.2 v23). The ridge of land must have belonged to Jacob and it would command respect from all who were there passing by.

- - - - - - - -

With bitterness archers attacked him; they shot at him with hostility. But his bow remained steady, his strong arms stayed supple, because of the Might One of Jacob. Genesis ch.49 v23-24.

When Jacob who was old blesses his sons he said, 'Gather round me so that I can tell you what will happen to your situation'. The warlike Ephramites would proved victorious in battle (see Joshua ch.17 v18). They were close to the River Jordan from the Dead Sea to the Sea of Galilee and close to the Philistines cities. This was important to protect Israel from Ammon, Aram and the Philistines.

Their bow became steady and they could fight back. Their hostility was evident (see Judges ch.11 v4-23). Later they had serious problems with Ben-Hadad (see 1 Kings ch.20 v1-34).

- - - - - - -

Take up your positions round Babylon, all you who draw a bow. Shoot at her! Spare no arrows, for she has sinned against the Lord. Shoot against on every side! She surrenders, her towers fall, her walls are torn down. Jeremiah ch.50

The sword, spear, javelin, sling and battle axe as they were fighting one to one. Each one faced the other. But the bow and arrow could shoot a long way off.

Look an army is coming up from the north; a great nation and many kings are being stirred up from the ends of the earth. They are armed with bows and spears; they are cruel and without mercy. They sound like the roaring sea as they ride on their horses; they come like men in battle formation to attack you, O daughter of Babylon. Jeremiah ch.50 v41-42

This is what it was like for the great nation. They could aim with bows, this is the force of Babylon, placed in her proud walls. The only way that they could shoot at her was with bows and arrows. Then they broke down her walls and towers and her king was slain (see Daniel ch.5).

Art

There is little evidence in the Old Testament on which to build a picture of the work of Israelites art. Palestine was occupied by mixed peoples and conditions, so it is impossible to distinguish the art from the nations around them.

The Israelites did as Moses instructed and asked the Egyptians for articles and silver and gold and for clothing. Exodus ch.12 v35

There is nothing in the book of Genesis, but when the Israelites moved into Egypt to escape the famine they settled in the region of Goshen, close to the land of Palestine. Over the years, they were eventually slaves working for the Egyptian Pharaoh. When the plagues struck Egypt they were moved back into Palestine.

Before they went, Moses asked the Egyptians to give them products that they could use, including gold and silver. They could use them for art.

Aaron answered them, "Take off the gold ear rings that your wives, you sons and your daughters are wearing, and bring them to me." So all the people took off their gold ear-rings that your wives, your sons and your daughter are wearing, and bring them to me." So all the people took off their ear-rings and brought them to Aaron. He took what they handed him and made it into an idol cast in the shape of a calf, fashioning it with a tool. Exodus ch.32 v2-4

While they were travelling with the sheep, they had tents to house the wives and children. It was a slow journey over several Wildernesses of Paran, Shur and Zin. They didn't want to go to the two main routes up into Palestine because they were slaves and didn't want to fight to get to the Promised Land. They were indeed separate but they had tools to use for ear-rings in the desert.

While they were in the Mount Sinai, where the Egyptians used to mine turquoise and copper. Moses went up to the mountain and he stayed a long while (see Exodus ch.32 v1). The Israelites might have thought he was dead. The gold earrings that they were using for their wives, daughters and sons were made up into an idol. It quite fashionable to make gold into earrings and there's a lot of gold from the Egyptians. We are not told what it was, but gold earrings must have been light not heavy. The Israelites had done was to work the gold and so, Aaron made it into a calf. He had to have a cast mould to melt it down and then shape it with a tool.

- - - - - - -

The Lord has filled Bezalel with the Spirit of God, giving him great wisdom, ability, and expertise in all kinds of craft. He has a master craftsman, expert in working with gold, silver, and bronze. He is skilled in engraving and mounting gemstones and in carving wood. He is a master at every craft. And the Lord has given both him and Oholiab son of Ahisamach, of the tribe of Dan, the ability to teach their skills to others. The Lord has given them special skills as engravers, designers, embroiderers in blue, purple, and scarlet thread on fine linen cloth, and weavers. They excel as craftsmen and as designers. "The Lord has gifted Bezalel, Oholiab, and the other skilled craftsmen with wisdom and ability to perform any task involved in building the sanctuary. Let them construct and furnish the Tabernacle, just as the Lord has commanded." Exodus ch.35 v31 – ch.36 v1 (NLT)

God has chosen Bezalel and Ohaliab, he has given him great wisdom, ability and expertise in all kind of craft. He has given them the ability to train others in their skills. For example:

Metals - with gold, silver and bronze.

Stonework - to mount gemstones.

Woodwork - to carve and shape wood.

Curtains - engravers, embroiders and weavers.

They would excel as craftsmen and designers. To construct and furnish the Tabernacle, the Tent of Meeting. Where God would meet the Israelites and direct them to follow in his ways. It was the tent where Moses went and sought with God. Nobody was allowed to enter the Tent of Meeting except for the priests.

Bezalel made the lampstand of pure, hammered gold. He made the entire lampstand and its decorations of one piece—the base, center stem, lamp cups, buds, and petals. Exodus ch.37 v17 (NLT)

Consider the lampstand: he made it of pure gold all in one piece. That was a significant effort to hammer it out, thinking of all cups, buds and petals. Nobody could say that the Israelites were backward in the arts. They even trained other people, they did it in the Wilderness of Paran.

Attacked

To act against someone with violence or to criticise mercilessly.

Now Cain said to his brother Abel, "Let's go out to the field." While they were in the field, Cain attacked his brother Abel and killed him. Genesis ch.4 v8

The two sons of Adam, Abel kept flocks of sheep but Cain worked with the soil. They each produced a gift to God. Abel brought fat from the lamb and Cain brought fruits of the soil. God looked on Abel with favour.

Why? The contrast is not between an offering of plant life and an offering of animal life, but between a careless, thoughtless offering and a choice generous offering. The motivation and attitude of heart are all important to God.

So Cain killed Abel, this was an evil thing that he did. He was uncaring and reckless. He tried to explain to God that he hadn't done anything wrong.

This is why God cursed Adam because his son would kill his brother. He killed his brother in the field, away from his home. He didn't say, 'You have done a better thing than I have done'. He killed him with a calculated intent. The first murder was especially vicious because it was committed with deliberate deceit. A striking illustration of the fall of Adam. So the curse would fall on people with suddenness and woeful impetuous.

Cain means 'metal-smith' he was used to working with metal. It is certainly not true that metal came later with the bronze age. It was there in the beginning, for Cain was used to working with metal. This is why he killed him, it was a sword or a sharp arrow and not strangled his brother.

- - - - - - -

Lamech said to his wives, "Adah and Zillah, listen to me; wives of Lamech, hear my words. I have killed a man for wounding me, a young man for injuring me. If Cain is avenged seven times, then Lamech seventy-seven times." Genesis

Everyone new what he did, he attacked a man. Even Lamech, the seventh from Adam in the line of Cain (see Genesis ch.4 v17-18). He killed a young man for injuring Lamech. Why? This is the second death and it is malicious. A young man for wounding another man. Because he talked about it, he tried to explain it away. Lamech did more evil than Cain did and he mentioned it to his wives.

Violent and wanton destruction of human life by one who claimed independence of God by taking vengeance with his own hands. Lamech proudly claimed to be nature of his destiny, thinking that by his sons, by their own achievements, would redeem themselves from the curse of Cain. But it was wrong to do so, for attacking a man who wounded me. He didn't say, 'I was on the point of death, he overpowered me and I had to do it'.

- - - - - - -

I did not bring you animals torn by wild beasts; I bore the loss myself. Genesis ch.31 v39

Jacob explained to Laban that he had been left out in all weathers looking after Laban's sheep. The heat consumed me in the daytime and the cold at night. You changed my wages ten times, and you would have sent me away empty-handed. Twenty years I have toiled for you for your daughters (see Genesis ch.31 v40-42).

He said, 'I bore the loss myself, I made it up for you'. Laban's sheep and goats have not miscarried, nor have I eaten rams from your flocks. If the wild beasts, a lion or a bear (see 1 Samuel ch.17 v34-35) had taken one of his animals Jacob had killed it.

But he had taken away most of Laban's sheep by cunning exploitation through the water they were drinking; he took fresh branches from the trees and peeled of the bark and put it into the water (see Genesis ch.30 v37-43). It was a cunning plan to take most of his spotted sheep away, it wasn't an attack by name, it was an attack by cheating and double-dealing.

- - - - - - -

Then they set out, and the terror of God fell upon the towns all around them to so that no-one pursued them. Genesis ch.35 v5

Jacob had a daughter called Dinah. But she was molested and raped by Shechem, the son of Hamor the Hivite. He wanted to marry her. But the sons of Jacob were very angry about it they were filled with grief and fury (see Genesis ch.34 v2-7). Eventually Simeon and Levi, two of Dinah's brothers attached the unsuspecting city and killed every male who they thought was circumcised; they were very sore. They seized the plunder all their woman and children, everything in their houses and took it away (see Genesis ch.34 v25-29).

No-one came after them, the terror of God fell upon all the towns around them and they moved away to Bethel. They two of them said, "Should he have treated our sister like a prostitute." Shechem's crime, though serious as it was, hardly warranted such brutal and extensive retaliation.

- - - - - - -

Gad will be attacked by a hand of raiders for he will attack them at their heels. Genesis ch.49 v19

Located east of the River Jordan valley, the descendants of Gad were vulnerable to raids by the Moabites to the south (see Judges ch.3 v12-14; Judges ch.6 v1-6). The Moabites were located behind the Dead Sea with the mountains passing through their country.

Gad decided it would be better to remain outside of the Promised Land with the very large herds and flocks. He saw that the lands of Jazer and Gilead were suitable for livestock (see Numbers ch.32 v1). This was the Transjordan Tribes but they struggled with Moab to the south and Ammon in the north.

Jacob blesses his sons before he died, but he didn't know which way Gad had planned, so he promised that Gad will rise up and not be defeated.

Avenged

Avenged to take vengeance on someone to repay.

They will be places of refuge from the avenger, so that a person accused of murder may not die before he stands trial before the assembly. Numbers ch.35 v12

Murder was a serious occurrence, so God had one of the Ten Commandments (see Exodus ch.20 v13). The relatives of the one who died would come after the person and would strike him down. This is a premeditated and deliberate act of revenge, but it was allowable to rid the land of murder.

But not when a person who had no vested interest and did not intend to harm him, it was an accident. The person who manages to escape the relatives to the nearest city of refuge. Where a person of unintentional manslaughter might escape blood revenge, this will have to be determined by a judge. Further, the accused man had to remain in the city of refuge until the death of the high priest when there would be a general amnesty (see Numbers ch.35 v28). It was a serious matter.

- - - - - - -

For the time has come for me to avenge my people, to ransom them from their oppressors. I was amazed to see that no one intervened to help the oppressed. Isaiah ch.63 v4-5 (NLT)

God's righteousness and holiness resulted in his wrath against the sinner. He would come to bring justice on his enemies and rescue them from their oppressors. Nobody will come to help so God had to do it on his own.

This is true where the person had a long life living on this earth. But God has mighty powers and is strong and able to confront the sinner, he will avenge the wicked before the day of judgement.

Then the kings of the earth the princes, the generals, the rich, the mighty and every slave and every free man hid in caves and among the rocks of the mountains. Revelation ch.6 v15

Every man from the princes to every slave hid in the rocks and caves because of the wrath of God. The wrath of God is able to single you out and affect you. Like the people affected with breathing difficulties.

I call on the Lord in my distress, and he answers me. Save me, O Lord, from lying lips and from deceitful tongues. Psalm ch.120 v1-2

The tongue is also a fire, a world of evil among the parts of the body. It corrupts the whole person, sets the whole course of his life on fire, and is itself set of fire by hell. James ch.2 v6

It is the tongue that makes great boasts and marks the wicked person out, where God is avenged for the evil person. The tongue is an evil part of man it speaks from the heart but says things that really hurt others.

Astrology

Astrology is a form of divination.

Divination is roughly the attempt to discern events that are distant in time or space, that consequently cannot be perceived by normal means. Astrology draws conclusions from the position of the sun, moon and planets in relation to the zodiac and to one another.

When you look up to the sky and see the sun, the moon and the stars - all the heavenly array - do not be enticed into bowing down to them and worshipping things the Lord your God has apportioned to all the nations under heaven. Deuteronomy ch.4 v19

The sun, moon and stars to give light on the earth, to separate the day from the night, to separate the seasons from one another (see Genesis ch.1 v14-19). You don't worship such things. God has prepared for us to work out the day and the night and seasons. This is why he did it to shelter and protect us.

For instance, they might serve other gods or worship the sun, the moon, or any of the stars—the forces of heaven—which I have strictly forbidden. When you hear about it, investigate the matter thoroughly. If it is true that this detestable thing has been done in Israel, then the man or woman who has committed such an evil act must be taken to the gates of the town and stoned to death. Deuteronomy ch.17 v3-5 (NLT)

If a man or woman worships what was made by God, like the 'the sun, moon or any of the stars'. An Israelite living among you, in any one of your towns, if it is true, then the judges must decide and investigate properly. What is done is detestable and evil, the person who has done this must be stoned to death outside the city walls.

It is strictly forbidden by God. Taking away from the Lord the worship that rightly belong to him, it is an idol and that must be dealt with. The worship must be to the Lord God and him alone. It is dangerous thinking that doesn't matter, it really does.

- - - - - - -

The houses in Jerusalem and those of the kings of Judah will be defiled like this place, Topheth – all the houses where they burned incense on the roofs to all the starry hosts and poured out drink offerings to other gods. Jeremiah ch.19 v13

Astrology is an idol, like the 'starry hosts'. All the houses and those of the kings of Judah will be defiled. The kings of Judah had built pagan altars on the roof of the palace in Jerusalem (see 2 Kings 23 v10-12). This involved all the people and not just the king. Astrology gave rise to each of the people, they wanted to know what will happen.

God is not pleased with what they had been doing; turning to astrology and asking for the 'signs' to take place. It will be even worse, everybody will be doing it, even the judges. The judges will be responsible and nobody could die outside the city walls. The place is evil and God hates it with a passion that could not even be imagined.

You have lifted up the shrine of your king, the pedestals of your idols, the star of your god – which you made for yourselves. Therefore I will send you into exile beyond Damascus says the Lord, whose name is God Almighty. Amos ch.5 v26-27.

You have lifted up the shrine of Molech and the star of your god Rephan, the idols you made to worship. Therefore I will send you into exile beyond Babylon. Acts ch.7 v43

God said, 'You will be sent into exile for what you have done'. The word 'exile' means all the astrology paper, symbols on it, the charts, the events will be left behind to be burnt (see 2 Chronicles ch.36 v19). People will be on their own under guard, nothing will be taken away and certainly not astrology, you will be stripped and naked (see Isaiah ch.20).

This is what happens when astrology takes over. The astrology could not have predicted or imagined all this. Men and women chained together going into exile under a cruel, barbaric empire. Astrology can't foretell the future, God can and has done it in the Bible.

Bricks

Bricks is a lump of mud or clay.

Bricks are usually rectangular, sun-dried or kiln-baked. The commonest building material of the ancient Biblical world. At first moulded by hand, then bricks began to be made with open rectangular, wooden moulds. The mud was mixed with sand, chopped straw and the bricks struck-off in long rows and left to dry out.

Brick-kiln: bricks and were the cheapest material, but were not specially durable in rainy weather. The brick-kiln or rather 'burnt' were especially lasting and hard-wearing because it was fired by the flames.

- - - - - - -

They said to each other, "Come let us make bricks and bake them thoroughly." They used brick instead of stone, and bitumen for mortar. Genesis ch.11 v3

After the flood had wiped out all of the people, then the sons of Noah propagated and expanded the land of the middle east. Ham was in Egypt, Shem was in Arabia and Japeth in Turkey. They each had a common mission to build a Tower of Babel in Shinar. They were one basic language and a common speech and they got on well with each other.

They used bricks and to bake them thoroughly in the sun, with moulds. The mortar used was tar or bitumen. Interesting they used brick rather than stones. Bricks are easier to use but stones need quarrying.

Before the flood, stones were more widely used and there was work done in all the countries, not just the middle-east. Stones were heavy and they didn't have any equipment to aid manufacture to help to get the stones perfectly straight. Because of the flood wiped out the work they had been doing up until now.

As it happened, the valley of the Dead Sea was filled with tar pits. Genesis ch.14 v10 (NLT)

The Tower of Babel was enormous, the bricks were used in construction, one brick layered on top of another with bitumen for mortar. Before the flood there was no mortar used, the stones would be so close together there was no room between them and the stones were so massive in size. The Lord watched and decided that the Tower of Babel was not a good idea.

God scattered them all over the earth and confused their language. The building was never finished because they couldn't understand each other. He had other ideas to get them to separate over the earth (see Genesis ch.11 v9).

- - - - - - -

They made their lives bitter with hard labour in brick and mortar and with all kinds of work in the fields; in all their hard labour the Egyptians used them ruthlessly. Exodus ch.1 v14

While the Israelites were in Egypt the Pharaoh didn't remember what Joseph had done. How he managed to get the grain stored up in the good years and saved the people from the years of famine. The Pharaoh made the lives of the Israelite so hard so they were the sad, victims of slavery.

Doing work with bricks and mortar. It is bending down on the floor, treading out the clay to make the bricks and it is very hard to do that. They were using the bricks with mortar, which will have to be either mixed up, or dug out from the ground. It is very unyielding and inflexible work, especially in the sun with the heat. Then after Moses and Aaron went to Pharaoh. He said to his slave drivers:

"You are no longer to supply the people with straw for making bricks; let them go and gather their own straw. But require them to make the same number of bricks as before; don't reduce the quota." Exodus ch.5 v7-8

The Pharaoh decided that the Israelites were lazy and they wanted to go off to sacrifice to their god. He didn't give the straw to be used, he made the Israelites find it for the mortar. If you are using clay and mixed with straw to get the bricks to hold together, but he instructed the slave drivers not to let the bricks be less than the quota. He directed that the slaves had to make the same bricks as before. It is double the work and the people cried out to the Lord.

- - - - - - -

Then the Lord said to Moses and Aaron, "Take handfuls of soot from a brick kiln, and have Moses toss it into the air while Pharaoh watches. The ashes will spread like fine dust over the whole land of Egypt, causing festering boils to break out on people and animals throughout the land." Exodus ch.9 v8-9 (NLT)

The use of a brick kiln makes the bricks very hard, it will be useful for when the bad weather will arrive. But most of the work will be dry, the rainfall is not expected to be much. Egypt is 96% desert but only 4% usable land where the River Nile flows into the Mediterranean Sea. The use of the brick kiln is going to make the bricks very hard, whereas they will be used for many years and still hold their shape.

'The ashes will spread like a fine dust', and they will have a fire underneath the bricks. It makes it easier than relying on the sun. The inside of the bricks will get the same heat as the top ones. There will be a lot of brick kilns in one place to help get the wood stored together. The Egyptians managed the fire and the Israelites slaves swept out the ashes. It will be hard work for the slaves.

- - - - - - -

All of Mount Sinai was covered with smoke because the Lord had descended on it in the form of fire. The smoke billowed into the sky like smoke from a brick kiln, and the whole mountain shook violently. Exodus ch.19 v18 (NLT)

It will take a quantity of heat to manage the brick kiln work and the Israelite slaves would be covered with the heat of the sun and the soot from the kiln.

Think of the steam locomotive engine firemen shovelling in coal, not once but several times as the train went along. The fireman had to shovel in the coal from the tender to the firebox. He will be dripping wet and coal dust would come on him. The clothing was covered with dust. Moving soot is the same problem as dust from a brick kiln.

Small wonder that the 'mountain shook violently' while God was coming to see what they were doing. God would know everything that the slaves had been doing.

- - - - - -

He took a great quantity of plunder from the city and brought out the people who were there, consigning them to labour with saws and iron picks and axes, and he made them work at brickmaking. He did this to all the Ammonite towns. 2 Samuel ch.12 v30-31

The Ammonite towns, not one town, but several towns across the River Jordan. King David decimated them, he managed to get the surviving inhabitants and made them work at brickmaking. Consigning them to labour with saws and pick and axes and not a very nice duty to perform. Men and women were to be treated the same way.

Victorious kings during the time of the middle east often used prisoners of war as menial labourers in royal building projects. It was useful in making them as slaves, do menial work to forget them not to build up a large force, they took away their swords, spears and shields. This was how they constructed palaces and rooms for the rich.

- - - - - -

Get ready for the siege! Store up water! Strengthen the defences! Go into the pits to trample clay, and pack it into moulds, making bricks to repair the walls. Nahum ch.3 v14 (NLT)

In the prophet Nahum's time, when he prophesied about the fall of Ninevah. He speaks of the end of the Babylonian empire, 'Get ready for the siege'. It is the work to make bricks to shore up the walls of the city. Like:

Go into the pits, dig out the clay.

Trample clay, prepare the clay for the bricks.

Pack it into moulds, prepare the moulds for use.

This is useful, it sorts out the work of the brick-maker. How he dug out clay and he used moulds for the bricks. But he didn't fire the bricks in a kiln, he used the bricks as they were to pack out his walls. He didn't bother to use hard bricks, because the enemy would break and smash the walls down.

Several centuries have come and gone, but the work of the bricks will still be useful to replace stone. The brick kiln cannot be used as there is not much time, the work of the bricks will have to do when the enemy comes up to the walls of the city. The stone will last forever but the bricks will underpin and brace the walls.

Building

To construct a building. It doesn't means bricks and stones, but the whole building must be made or completed.

From that land he went to Assyria, where he build Nineveh ... which is between Nineveh (and four others) ... that is the great city. Genesis ch.10 v11-12

After the flood, Noah sons had a table of nations, each of them had descendants. Cush built the first centres of his kingdom were in Shinar located in southern Mesopotamia within the Fertile Crescent. Assyria and Babylon will be built by him.

Fertile Crescent: the rich soil which is located from Egypt to Syria. The edge of the Mediterranean Sea and the desert in Jordan means that the affluent ground is the ideal for sheep and crops. This is the Promised Land that the people in Israel should go to, it was a land for the Covenant by the Lord God.

The work of building a great city. The walls kept the people in and they were thick, solid structures. We know from the archaeological excavations that these cities lasted over many years. They were constructed with stone braced together with ramparts. A city has many buildings each constructed with bricks and mud, with beams holding the roof up, it might have been reeds not timber. Each time a builder constructed a city it was not basic mud huts, so the families could be protected while they were there. The work in a great city would have stables for the horses, towers to look out for the enemy, palace for the ruler and trading houses or shops where the people could meet.

Building a city required expertise and planning. Constructing the workers and a whole lot of skilful, clever work.

Now Nineveh was a very important city - a visit required three days. Jonah ch.3 v3

Nineveh had more than 120,000 people (see Jonah ch.4 v11). It took three days for Jonah to reach all the people. It wasn't a small city. How long did it take to construct the walls? Cush a son of Ham built the city Babylon and Ninevah (see Genesis ch.10 v11), and several more cities he constructed and built.

So the Lord scattered them from there over all the earth, and they stopped building the city. This is why it is called Babel – because the Lord confused the language of the whole world. Genesis ch.11 v8-9

Before the Lord confused there language and they started by constructing a great city called Babel. Everyone worked together and they were intended to build a tower that reached to the heavens. They wanted to have structure that the world would be proud of. To take its destiny in its man-made efforts to try to seize its unrestrained rebellion against God. This is why God caused man to confuse their language so they didn't understand each other.

The building was very good and even God came down to look at the building (see Genesis ch.11 v5). They pulled together, each man had a work to do, constructing the earth, bricks, furnace, piles to reach the top, ladders and such. They acted as one and it was a ziggurat. Was square at the base and had sloping sides, stepped sides that led to upward to a small shrine at the top. It was carefully and properly designed.

- - - - - - -

This is an inventory of the materials used in building the Tabernacle of the Covenant. The Levites compiled the figures, as Moses directed, and Ithamar son of Aaron the priest served as recorder. Exodus ch.38 v21 (NLT)

There was gold, silver and bronze materials used by the Levites under the work for the building of the Tabernacle of the Covenant. The work was directed by Ithamar, son of Aaron. They completed the construction of the Lord who had given the work to Moses. The action, direction and instruction while he was there in the Mount of Sinai.

Since were 3,000 shekels in a talent. The total amount was used:

Gold was 29 talents and 730 shekels.

Sliver was 100 talents and 1,175 shekels.

Bronze was 70 talents ad 2,400 shekels.

Its a lot of precious metals which were to be used to add to the building. The construction used gold, silver and bronze work to add to what the Levites were doing (see Exodus ch.38 v21-31).

- - - - - - -

David finished building his palace and the temple of the Lord, and the wall around Jerusalem. 1 Kings ch.3 v1

King Solomon (rather than David) had constructed his palace, God's temple and the walls around his city. The stone foundations were often surmounted by brick walls. The enormous city walls consisted of a stone strong footing, the outer battered face smoothed over with plaster to keep horses at a distance, with thick brick walls, sometimes containing chambers inside them.

Solomon palace, a hundred cubits long, fifty wide and thirty high, with four rows of cedar columns supporting trimmed cedar beams. Its windows were placed high in sets of three facing each other. All the doorways had rectangular frames. He made a colonnade fifty cubits long and thirty wide. In front of it was a portico and there were pillars and an overhanging roof (see 1 Kings ch.7 v1-6). It took Solomon thirteen years to build this palace.

That is his palace and the work of building the temple of the Lord he had spent seven years building the temple of God at 60 cubits long, 20 wide and 30 high (see 1 Kings ch.6 v2). In building the temple, only blocks were used at the quarry (see 1 Kings ch.6 v7). Roofing it with beams and cedar planks (see 1 Kings ch.6 v9).

He constructed a large amount of building works. Much wealth flowed into the royal treasuries and Solomon came to be known the one of the great builders in the history of that time. The remains of fortifications and public buildings from the time of Solomon are not listed in the Bible, but work has uncovered his supreme efforts. Solomon used construction materials from the Phoenicia, transporting them with their ships.

I undertook great projects, I built houses for myself and planted vineyards. I made gardens and parks and planted all kinds of fruit trees in them. I made reservoirs to water groves of flourishing trees ... I became greater by far than anyone else of Jerusalem before me. Ecclesiastes ch.2 v4-6, v9

King Solomon undertook great projects at a very considerable cost (see 2 Chronicles ch.10 v3-4). He used his people as servants, but fortunately he didn't treat them like slaves (see 2 Chronicles ch.8 v1-10).

- - - - - - -

So in the ninth year of Zedekiah's reign, on the tenth day of the tenth month; Nebuchadnezzar king of Babylon marched against Jerusalem with his whole army. He encamped outside the city and build siege works all around it. The whole city was kept under siege until the eleventh year of King Zedekiah. By the ninth day of the fourth month the famine in the city had become so severe that there was not enough food for the people to eat. Then the city wall was broken through. 2 Kings ch.25 v1-4

Over 18 months the city wall held against all of the Babylon army. King Nebuchadnezzar built siege works against it, but still the walls remained. They were indeed thick, built with stones at the base and kept out the Babylon remaining soldiers. The who army under king Nebuchadnezzar was trying to enter it, but he couldn't get through even the gates remained shut and barred so tightly.

This is what the city of Jerusalem was like. Magnificent high walls protected those inside.

Families

Families like household all those who lived in the same house. For example: parents, children, servants and slaves.

God said, "I will bless those who bless you and curse those who treat you with contempt. All the families on earth will be blessed through you." Genesis ch.12 v3 (NLT)

Abraham was promised that God would protect him for his life on earth. But the promise of God was that of his descendants should be protected as well.

God was with the family of Abraham however long it would take, he would be in the land of Palestine associated with the temple of God until the end of the age. Why did he do it? God was bringing a new humanity into being of whom Abraham was the father (see Genesis ch.17 v5-8), just as Adam and Noah were fathers of the fallen human race. He would bless Abraham, provided he obeyed God's commands and instructions.

God said, "I have singled him out so that he will direct his sons and their families to keep the way of the Lord by doing what is right and just. Then I will do for Abraham all that I have promised." Genesis ch.18 v19 (NLT)

God decided that his sons and their families should keep the Lord 'by doing what is right and just'. This was a further instruction for God's plan (see Deuteronomy ch.28). The descendants of Abraham didn't do it, so God sent his prophets but they ignored them, so God exiled his people away from the Promised Land (see Daniel ch.9 v1-19).

The Lord has kept his promise to Abraham (see Romans ch.11 v25-32), for God's gift and his call are irrevocable. But the apostle Paul still maintains that as far as the gospel is concerned they are enemies on your account, because they are not willing to accept Jesus Christ as their Messiah, but some indeed do, including the priests.

- - - - - - -

God has sent me ahead of you to keep you and your families alive and to preserve many survivors. So it was God who sent me here, not you! And he is the one who made me an adviser to Pharaoh—the manager of his entire palace and the governor of all Egypt. Genesis ch.45 v7-8 (NLT)

Joseph, Jacob's son who was deserted and sold by his brothers into slavery and sent down to Egypt. He spent several years in the royal prison, serving care of the people who offended Pharaoh. He had a gift for understanding dreams. Therefore Pharaoh had a dream which the wise men couldn't answer. Joseph was able to do it and saved his people under the worst famine that would come upon Egypt and Palestine.

It was God 'who sent me here'. Joseph didn't fault his brothers for their treachery, but he was there in Egypt under the worst starvation for seven years. One or two years the famine would come hard upon the people but seven years, it would take a long while for the people to recover. He saved Egypt from the famine but he left the people destitute, but not the priests because they had a special arrangement with the Pharaoh.

Then get your father and all of your families, and return here to me. I will give you the very best land in Egypt, and you will eat from the best that the land produces. Genesis ch.45 v18 (NLT)

The family was very important, so Joseph taught his brother to say that they were sheep farmers (see Genesis ch.46 v34), this was the worst thing that could happen. A place away from the River Nile where the Egyptians should plant grain so the sheep would munch the seed when it grows up. So the people were allocated to the land of Goshen, the best that Egypt could provide. An area rich with grass and the four rivers flowing into the Mediterranean Sea and there was a lake. Why would they go back to Palestine with all the hills?

Joseph thought they would be comfortable and have the 'best of the land'. The families would trace their roots back to Abraham, it was a refuge and a separate option for the people that God had selected. The first chapters of the book of 1 Chronicles ch.1 - ch.9, indicated that it was very important. We notice that after the Judah had gone into exile, the same thought was there with the listing of the people who came back (see Ezra ch.2; Nehemiah ch.7). The genealogy of the Messiah was recognised by the author from Abraham to Jesus (see Matthew ch.1 v1-17).

Fear

Fear a painful emotion excited by danger.

Then ten of Joseph's brothers went down to buy grain from Egypt. But Jacob did not send Benjamin, Joseph's brother, with the others, because he was afraid that some harm might come to him. Genesis ch.42 v3–4

Rachel had died giving birth to Benjamin (see Genesis ch.35 v16-19), so Jacob had lost Joseph and did not want to lose his other precious son. It was a journey of some 300 miles to Egypt going down the road through the Wilderness of Paran. There were 10 brothers going down to Egypt, but they were shepherds away from the house looking after the sheep. It was probably some wild animals or like snakes and scorpions that Jacob feared most in the desert or wilderness. There is no medical facility to get treatment.

- - - - - - -

I will grant peace in the land, and you will lie down and no-one will make you afraid. I will remove savage beasts from the land, and the sword will not pass through your country. Leviticus ch.26 v6

On the way from Goshen the Israelites moved out, not on Via Maris path because they were heading to Palestine and the Egyptians had stations and fortresses along the way. The Israelite slaves couldn't fight back because they were not used to fighting. They were slaves and had Egyptian masters treating them badly; they waited until further orders came along. The Israelites headed south passing down through the Mount of Sinai.

God reminded them where they were going to the Promised Land and he would make sure that they had peace. What is peace like?

Peace: means an absence of trouble (see John ch.14 v27). Not as the world gives peace. It is more than that (see John ch.20 v19-20). Jesus gives us a calm, quiet stillness, the Holy Spirit reminds us that we are on a journey to look for the kingdom that will appear (see Hebrews ch.11). We are not afraid, but a undisturbed, restful place where we can be at peace.

As the world is full of violence and mayhem so the prophet Elijah heard a gentle whisper (see 1 Kings ch.19 v11-12). He heard it, but the outside noise would be such that was going on around him. It was a quiet whisper of sound that the Holy Spirit makes in your mind or heart.

- - - - - - -

This very day I will begin to put the terror and fear of you on all the nations under heaven. They will hear reports of you and will tremble and will be in anguish of you. Deuteronomy ch.2 v25

On this day God will put in the minds of the people 'terror and fear' that the Israelites are coming with their sovereign God, who lights up their way with the pillar of fire and cloud. They had already reached the Promised Land but they had to go through Moab. Because of the Dead or Salt Sea on the west and the wilderness of the east.

The king of Moab was terrified because there were so many people, he went and called Balaam to curse them (see Numbers ch.22 v1-6). He couldn't do it because the Lord had protected them. The fear of the Lord is more powerful and effective. Moab saw the people and quaked in fear at what they could do.

The king said, "This horde is going to lick up everything around us, as an ox licks up the grass of the field." Numbers ch.22 v4

After that, when Joshua went over the River Jordan to Jericho all the city was secure and nobody went in or out (Joshua ch.6 v1). The terror of fear of you will pass over to the kings and cities. They will be unnerved and petrified of you.

You saw with you own eyes the great trials, the miraculous signs and wonders, the mighty hand and the outstretched arm, with which the Lord your God brought you out. The Lord your God will do the same to all the peoples you now fear. Deuteronomy ch.7 v19

Remember what God did as you were going out of slavery, the troubles he brought upon the Egyptians. He for arranged Moses and Aaron to lead you out with all your gold and silver and all your herds of sheep. This is what he can do with the hail, the flies and frogs in Egypt. He is an Almighty God and he can do wonders without anybody being around.

It is important that you realise that the journey out of Egypt was not brought about because the people were righteous or good, but God brought them out and promised them they could have the Promised Land for themselves. It is God who made the difference while they were in the Wilderness of Paran.

You forefathers who went down into Egypt were seventy in all, and now the Lord your God has made you as numerous as the stars in the sky. Deuteronomy ch.10 v22

God strengthened them and made them mighty and can handle with Joshua. Moses died and he commissioned Joshua to go into Canaan (see Deuteronomy ch.31 v14).

- - - - - - -

The Lord your God will drive out those nations before you, little by little. You will not be allowed to eliminate them all at once, or the wild animals will multiply around you. But the Lord your God will deliver them over to you, throwing them into great confusion until they are destroyed. Deuteronomy ch.7 v22-23

The Israelites understood that God was there, but they didn't see him. He was there in the pillar of cloud or light (see Exodus ch.13 v21-22). The Israelites could pass by, or go by day and night.

When you come to the Promised Land you will not be able to eject all the Canaanites otherwise the wild animals will attack you. God was very kind to his family, he guarded them everyday. He was ready to help his people the Israelites rather then letting them occupy the land. He thought about the wild animals that were there, he knew about all of the animals, he made them.

- - - - - - -

There the Lord will give you an anxious mind, eyes weary with longing, and a despairing heart. You will live in constant suspense, filled with dread both night and day, never sure of your life. In the morning you will say, "If it were evening!" and in the evening, "if it only were morning!" – because of the terror that will fill you hearts and the sights that your eyes will see. Deuteronomy ch.28 v65-67

At the end of the prophet Moses life, he said to all the Israelites, 'You will have to obey God and all his commandments'. Otherwise, your children will carry on with the customs of the nations where they are going. They will carry on with the Baals and Ashtoreths, the idols with which the Canaanites practised and worshipped, leaving the Almighty God out.

The terror and fear of God will forsake you and you will have an 'anxious mind' worrying about what will happen to Israel and Judah. This is exactly what happened. In the countryside, they forgot about God and were exiled away from the Promised Land. Israel first under the Assyrian Empire, then Judah second under the Babylonian Empire.

They didn't realise what God had intended for them to do. If they served God he would bless them, if they didn't he would curse them. It is a solemn warning for us on this earth. If we leave God out and ignore him and do other things which he doesn't like, he will reject us and leave us to what is going to happen and it isn't very good. When Jesus came, God's own Son, bringing light into our world. They rejected him and crucified him on the cross. In the Promised Land he warned against the Pharisees who were supposed to bring help to the Temple, but they arrested him and handed him over to the Romans.

Jesus said, "You will hear of wars and rumour of wars ... nation will rise against nations and kingdoms against kingdoms. There will be famines and earthquakes in various places." Matthew ch.24 v6-8

The families will have to manage as best they can with what is going on around them. Many believers will be killed because of Jesus and many false prophets will appear and lead many astray (see Matthew ch.22 v9-11).

Food

Food nourishes the body and promotes growth and activity.

Then God said, "I give you every seed-bearing plant on the face of the whole earth and every tree that has fruit with seed in it. They will be yours for food. And to all the beasts of the earth and all the birds of the air and all the creatures that move on the ground - everything that has the breath of life in it - I give every green plant for food." Genesis ch.1 v29-30

God intended that everyone had food to live and grow. Man, animals and birds of the sky should feast on what God has provided. There was enough food for everyone for the whole earth was covered with plants and trees. This is why God decided to give the plants and trees room to survive before he made the creatures to eat from them.

Nowhere in the beginning there was famine or starvation, it wasn't there. Everything that God had provided was good for everyone to eat. But it was only vegetation, plants and berries.

- - - - - - -

The fear and dread of you will fall upon all the beasts of the earth and all the birds of the air, upon every creature that moves along the ground, and upon all the fish of the sea; they are given into your hands. Everything that lives and moves will be food for you. Just as I gave you the green plants, I now give you everything. Genesis ch.9 v3

Man and woman sinned against God and the whole system was changed. Men, animals, fish, plants and trees died. God created thorns and thistles and the whole earth was indeed ruined and spoiled (see Genesis ch.3 v16-19).

This is only after the flood. God wiped out all of the men and animals and birds because of the evil and violence that preceded it (see Genesis ch.6 v5-7). Noah and his family were saved by the ark who floated above the waters. God let on his ark, male and female animals and birds to be saved, so he didn't have to created them again. After the flood, God gave man everything to eat and not only the green plants.

This started the carnivorous process, and man and animal killed what all of them wanted to eat.

God said, "But you must not eat meat that has its lifeblood still in it. And for your lifeblood I will surely demand an accounting." Genesis ch.9 v4

This stresses the intimate relationship between blood and life. Life is the precious and mysterious gift of God (see Leviticus ch.17 v11). If an animal kills another person God will demand an accounting for this. Nobody, man and animal should harm come for a man for his lifeblood.

Is a serious thing, whether native-born or alien must still be held responsible. If a man hunts another animal it is first to be drained of its blood. On the ground it will be covered with earth. This is what God commanded man to do.

Whoever sheds the blood of man, by man shall his blood be shed; for in the image of God has God made man. Genesis ch.9 v6

Man is very important for in God's image, he has created and made him like the Lord. He is an unique and special being. If anyone kills another man, he would be killed for his blood that was shed. God will demand an accounting for the blood or life. It is forbidden by the Ten Commandments (see Exodus ch.20 v13). Which will come later when the Israelites went to Mount Sinai.

- - - - - - -

The Lord said to Moses and Aaron, Say to the Israelites: 'Of all the animals that live on land, these are the one you may eat: You may eat any animal that has a split hoof completely divided and that chews the cud ... Of all the creatures living in the water of the sea and the streams, you may eat any that have fins and scales ... These are the birds you are to detest and not eat because they are detestable ... All flying insects that walk on all fours and to be detestable to you' "Leviticus ch.11 v1-3, v9, v13, v20 and Deuteronomy ch.14 v1-21

All the creatures acceptable for human consumption, but the distinction between clean and unclean food to preserve the sanctity of Israel as God's holy people (see Leviticus ch.11 v44). The idea that certain animal life was considered unclean for health reasons is not really clear. Uncleanness typifies sin and defilement.

Israel's holiness was to be expressed in every aspect of her life to the extent that all life had a certain ceremonial quality. Because of who God is, what he has done, his people must dedicate themselves fully to him.

- - - - - - -

You must not eat the blood of any creature, because the life of every creature is in its blood; anyone who eats of it must be cut off. If one eats anything found dead or torn by wild animals must wash his clothes and bathe with water, and he will be ceremonial unclean till evening; then he will be clean. But if he does not wash his clothes and bath himself, he will be held responsible. Leviticus ch.17 v14–16

Why? Such animals would not have the blood drained from them and therefore would be forbidden. Here God's people are given instructions concerning personal relationships and morality reflecting God's holiness. Israel would be different from all the others nations whose lifestyle was completely immoral.

When the book of Deuteronomy was compiled. The Israelites were living close to the Promised Land coming from the Wilderness of Paran, they were about to enter Canaan. The reason is if you find a dead animal you must give it to an alien living in any of your towns.

Do not eat anything you find already dead. You may give it to an alien living in any of your towns, and he may eat of it, or you may sell it to a foreigner. But you are a people holy to the Lord your God. Deuteronomy ch.14 v21

Because of the prohibition against eating blood, since the dead animals blood would not be properly drained away and covered under the ground.

Game

Game is a sport of any kind or wild animals hunted for food.

Isaac loved Esau because he enjoyed eating the wild game Esau brought home, but Rebekah loved Jacob. Genesis ch.25 v28 (NLT)

Hostility between the Israelites (Jacob's descendants) and Edomites (Esau's descendants) became the rule rather than he exception. 'Beware of your friends; do not trust your brothers' (See Genesis ch.4 v8).

Because of Esau's hunting and Jacob's mother love brought evil into Isaac's house. Esau hunted wild game which Isaac loved but while he was gone out. Rebekah said, Go out to get me two choice goats that you can prepare for Isaac. Isaac was blind so he could not see, so he gave Jacob the blessing which he should have given to Esau the firstborn.

- - - - - - -

Lazy people don't even cook the game they catch, but the diligent make use of everything they find. Proverbs ch.12 v27 (NLT)

Lazy people are not able to lift the food from the dish to the mouth, it too much trouble, so miss a meal. Hunting game requires knowledge and patience. We know the hunt takes time, the animals will know that you are around, so you don't make a noise. Get downwind so they don't smell your clothes.

But idol and good-for-nothing people can't be bothered, find the weapons to go out and look. Subsequently they go hungry, because they are not able to go out looking for game to feed themselves.

A thief who is caught must pay in full for everything he stole. If he cannot pay, he must be sold as a slave to pay for his theft. Exodus ch.22 v3 (NLT)

That is why in the Old Testament the thief would be sold as a slave because God expected that everyone will be working. For looking after the sheep or working in the fields, sowing and harvesting. Man was expected to be out there to gather in for his livelihood (see Genesis ch.3 v17-19). He was expected to find employment for his family, God decided that man should go out in the fields and work hard. This is the curse that God decided to carry out (see Genesis ch.3 v17-19), the verses indicate sweating and painful toil.

- - - - - - -

But his own people have been robbed and plundered, enslaved, imprisoned, and trapped. They are fair game for anyone and have no one to protect them, no one to take them back home. Isaiah ch.42 v22 (NLT)

With the Assyrians and Babylonians empire they would be slaves again. Kept in prison, plundered and trapped with no one to help them. They would be fair game for anyone who wanted them to work hard. God would have abandoned them there in slavery but he would still be looking after them.

Haman was hanged for his part in the plot (see Esther ch.8 v7-8). But no one has the right to alter the king's Xerxes command can be revoked. So put another document in place of the first. The edict which granted the Jews in every city the right to assemble and protect themselves, to plunder the property of their enemies (see Esther ch.8 v11).

Hurt

Hurt to cause pain, damage or injure people.

Then Moses became very angry and said to the Lord, "Do not accept their grain offerings! I have not taken so much as a donkey from them, and I have never hurt a single one of them." Numbers ch.16 v15 (NLT)

Certain men rose up against the prophet Moses. There were 250 men well-known, community leaders who had been appointed members of the council. Well respected men, a figurehead and with authority over the masses.

Moses complained to God he hadn't even taken as much as a 'donkey from them', he was furious that these men were trying to take over the priesthood from Aaron. He said, 'I've never hurt anyone of them'. Moses was badly hurt that they should replace the priests.

The next day, Korah, Dathan and Abiram were close to their tents. The earth moved and swallowed them up, even their wives and children. Fire came out and destroyed the 250 men who were offering incense, because these men have treated the Lord with contempt. God had decided that the priesthood was Aaron and his sons work.

- - - - - - -

Then David took an oath before Jonathan and said, "Your father knows perfectly well about our friendship, so he has said to himself, 'I won't tell Jonathan—why should I hurt him?' But I swear to you that I am only a step away from death! I swear it by the Lord and by your own soul!" 1 Samuel ch.20 v3 (NLT)

David knew that an evil spirit had come upon king Saul as he was sitting in his house with his spear in his hand. While David was playing with his harp to calm him down. But things didn't go to plan for Saul.

King Saul was seeking David life because he knew that David would be king after him. But Jonathan protected David, he would give his life to his friend; They had a bond between them (1 Samuel ch.18 v1). King Saul knew about Jonathan love, but David was frightened because King Saul has used his spear in his house to pin David to the wall (1 Samuel ch.19 v10).

Consequently, David escaped with his life and king Saul was looking for him with his whole army around him. David had only 400 men as he started out (see 1 Samuel ch.22 v2) or later 600 men when he went to the Philistines (see 1 Samuel ch.30 v10).

- - - - - - -

He said this when they were few in number, a tiny group of strangers in Canaan. They wandered from nation to nation, from one kingdom to another. Yet he did not let anyone oppress them. He warned kings on their behalf: "Do not touch my chosen people, and do not hurt my prophets." Psalm ch.105 v12-15 (NLT)

God's saving acts on Israel's behalf from the granting of the Covenant (see Genesis ch.15 v18) to its ultimate fulfilment (see Joshua ch.21 v43-45). The song or recital produced by Moses in conjunction with the offering of firstfruits that the Lord your God has given to Israel, when you have settled in the Promised Land to make it yours (see Deuteronomy ch.26 v1-11).

It is interesting that he said, 'Do not hurt my prophets'. The words Stephen used against the Sanhedrin when he said, 'Was there ever a prophet your forefathers did not persecute?' (see Acts ch.7 v52). Even the prophets were not escaping suffering (see Hebrews ch.11 v32-38). The prophets spoke the words of God and they were hated for doing this. But the kings must 'not touch them'. They were protected by God for doing the Lord's work.

- - - - - - -

"They pour out liquid offerings to their other idol gods! Am I the one they are

hurting?" asks the Lord. "Most of all, they hurt themselves, to their own shame."
So this is what the Sovereign Lord says: "I will pour out my terrible fury on this
place. Its people, animals, trees, and crops will be consumed by the unquenchable
fire of my anger." Jeremiah ch.7 v18–20 (NLT)

Entire families participated in idolatrous worship. All nations suffer when God judges sinners (see Romans ch.8 5-8). The world turned to idols because of their sinful nature, they need something to construct, to build.

They turned away from God and made idols for worship; God would be very angry that they did this. Every night the galaxies shine in the sky and people would not be able to think that God created all the stars and there is no excuse for mankind, whoever they are (see Romans ch.1 v18-20).

For God does not enjoy hurting people or causing them sorrow. Lamentations ch.3 v33 (NLT)

God doesn't hurt anybody or causing them sorrow or grief. Man in his sinful nature has turned away from God. It is his own actions and practice that makes him vulnerable like, going to hell. Why should we have war? Why do we make things that explode? Like guns and weapons. We are all cousins together from Noah who saved the world by his ark. We are descendants from him, regardless of what we are doing in our own nations. We have a responsibility to provide food to each other, not war.

Music

Music the art of expression in sound, in melody and harmony. Including competition and playing.

His brother's name was Jubal; he was the father of all who play the harp and the flute. Genesis ch.4 v21

Only five generations down from Cain, who was the son of Adam (see Genesis ch.4 v17-18). Like his descendants: Enoch, Irad, Mehujael, Methushael and Lamech.

Lamech married two women, one named Adal and gave birth to Jabal, his brother's name was Jubal. He had musical instruments, including the harp and flute. The harp is made of wood and the flute is made of metal. The harp needs fine strings and the flute needs careful blowing.

They were intelligent, knowledgeable and practised daily, not like stone age men in caves. They worked with wood and metal, but they produced musical instruments. The fine work of Jubal who was the best of his kind. How did he manage this? Who taught him? How did he think about music?

- - - - - - -

Why did you run off secretly and deceive me? Why didn't you tell me, so that I could send you away with joy and singing to the music of tambourines and harps? Genesis ch.31 v27

As he fled earlier from Esau, Jacob fled from Laban. Jacob's devious dealings produced only hostility from Laban. Gilead is a fertile region south-east of the Sea of Galilee. That is where he was going with all his sheep but he would go slowly otherwise his sheep wouldn't keep up.

The harps are much smaller and with fewer strings than the harps ususally played today and Laban had tambourines.

- - - - - - -

Here this, you kings! Listen, you rulers! I will sing to the Lord, I will sing; I will make music to the Lord, the God of Israel. Judges ch.5 v3

The song was probably written by Deborah a prophetess and is thus one of the oldest poems in the Bible. It celebrates before the nations, the righteous acts of the Lord and of his warriors. They played it together as a chorus.

- - - - - - -

Saul's servants said to him, "A tormenting spirit from God is troubling you. Let us find a good musician to play the harp whenever the tormenting spirit troubles you. He will play soothing music, and you will soon be well again." 1 Samuel ch.16 v15-16 (NLT)

King Saul didn't follow exactly the Lord as he let the bad spirit trouble him, gave him wrong and evil thoughts. David speaks well, is a handsome man and the Lord is with him and he can play the harp. So everybody knows that David is a harp player and he is very good, so he is instructed to play for the king.

Not strum painfully on his harp, but the music is soothing to king Saul and the evil spirit left him alone. It is worth noting the harp plays well and listeners can relax and feel better. David understood what the harp can do. I think that he will play for his sheep in the early days (see 1 Samuel ch.16 v11).

Ornaments

Ornaments are anything to add grace or beauty and are intended for display.

From the beginning ornamentation has been used by mankind to adorn the objects which surround him in his or her daily life. When the intention is right the skill of a craftsmen is pleasing to God. That the carving of wood and ivory was done with great skill, weaving and embroidery reached a very high standard and the fine techniques in metal were well understood.

Zamech married two women ... Zillah also had a son, Tubal-Cain, who forged all kinds out of bronze and iron. Genesis ch.4 v19, v22

He was a descendant of Cain who was a specialist and forger, of bronze and iron. Iron and tin had to be dug out of the soil; bronze is a mixture of iron and tin. It was in common use before the patriarchal times (Abraham, Issac and Jacob and his sons).

Shafts more than 100 feet in depth have often been found in mines in Egypt. Tunnels, ventilated by shafts, were driven into hillsides, pillars being left in broad excavations to support the roof. Wedges and fire were used to split the rock and the ore was separated by crushing, washing and hand-picking. Smelting was usually done on the spot in clay crucibles using charcoal as primitive bellows. Such crucibles and slag heaps are found at many old sites.

Forging needs a hammer and a bench or a stone and bends the metal to be used for making other things, without breaking it. If it is forged the metal is stretched and it is used today for so many metals. It is harder to break and if you want to make a wheel, forging is the best idea. Forging needs skill and time to work the metal into the correct shape and it is generally done with heat to work the metal.

- - - - - - -

So make yourself an ark of cyprus wood; make rooms in it and coat it with pitch, inside and out. This is how you are to build it: The ark is to be 450 feet long, 75 feet wide and 45 feet high. Make a roof for it and finish the ark to within 18 inches of the top. Put a door in the side of the ark and make lower, middle and upper decks. Genesis ch.6 v14-16

God was displeased with the world he had formed, it was corrupt and full of violence (see Genesis ch.6 v11). He had decided that he was going to flood the earth, but he selected male and female pairs of the animals were to come into the ark to keep them alive with Noah. God said, 'Each kind of bird and creature, you are to feed them and store them away as food'. The flood lasted a very long time, 150 days (See Genesis ch.7 v24).

Noah completed the ark but he didn't say that it was impossible to carry it out. The ark was so big with three floors to be built. He had his family to work with him and this was a specialise construction. He understood that all the joints would be strong to carry the ark for a long time, not simply braced together. He knew about boat building. So even today, we have power tools and specialised equipment to bend the beams to shape, scaffolding to work off the ground. There's many more people to shape the craft, but he did it with only his sons. How could he have manage to cut the wood to shape? Brace it to follow the outlines of the boat? It was a massive exercise and he didn't have any drawings he worked from the ground upwards to level the boat. He had a opening for the boat which requires skill and accuracy. He covered the boat with pitch inside and out, he must have reached under the boat to do it. The ark was braced to allow for the uneven ground.

Noah was 600 years old, he was a very fit man (see Genesis ch.7 v11).

- - - - - - -

Then at last, when the camels had finished drinking, he took out a gold ring for her nose and two large gold bracelets for her wrists. Genesis ch.24 v22 (NLT)

Abraham was very rich (see Genesis ch.24 v1), and the servant even had 10 camels laden with presents.

The rich gifts bestowed on Rebekah and her family indicated the wealth of the household into which she was being asked to marry, far from her loved ones and homeland. The servant took 10 camels filled with 'good things' and went to the city of Nahor (see Genesis ch.24 v10) a route of about 250 miles north.

A gold ring weighing at least a beka (half a shekel) and gold bracelets weighing 10 shekels on Rebekah's arms.

- - - - - - -

Then the Lord said to Moses, see I have chosen Bezalel son of Uri, the son of Hur, of the tribe of Judah, and I have filled him with the Spirit of God, with skill, ability and knowledge in all kinds of crafts – to make artistic designs for work in gold, silver and bronze, to cut and set stones, to work in wood and to engage in all kinds of craftsmanship. Exodus ch.31 v1-5

The Lord has chosen Bezalel and filled him with the promise that he would make what Moses asked for when he was with the Lord God on Mount Sinai.

The ability to work as a skilled craftsman was a spiritual gift, to equip the person for a special service to God. The craftsmen had to work with metal, wood, stone and cloth. He was able to equip others to help (see Exodus ch.31 v6; ch.36 v1-2).

All the skilled men among the workmen made the tabernacle with ten curtains of finely twisted linen and blue, purple and scarlet yarn, with cherubim worked into them for a skilled craftsman. Exodus ch.36 v8

They made all the fine curtains to go around the Tent of Meeting. This was fine work, the 10 curtains were 28 cubits long and 4 cubits wide and they joined the curtains together to hide what is inside the tent (see Exodus ch.36 v9-10).

They made a ephod of gold, and of blue, purple and scarlet yarn, and of finely twisted linen. They hammered out thin sheets of gold and cut strands to be worked into the blue, purple and scarlet yarn and fine linen – the work of a skilled craftsman. Exodus ch.39 v2-3

They made woven garments for ministering in the sanctuary (see Exodus ch.39 v1). The ephod is a sleeveless vestment worn by the high priest. The breast piece with 12 precious stones in it to hold the front and the back of the ephod to the high priest's body (see Exodus ch.28 v15-30).

The work involved was skilled and properly carried out and lasted many years until king Solomon made the temple of the Lord in Jerusalem, when the Tent of Meeting was coming to an end of its life.

God said, I have not dwelt in a house from the day I brought the Israelite up out of Egypt to this day. I have been moving from place to place with a tent as my dwelling. 2 Samuel ch.7 v6

We don't know what happened to the Tent of Meeting.

Sowing

Sowing is to scatter seed to put it in the ground to let it grow.

Then God said, "Let the land produce vegetation: seed-bearing plants and trees on the land that bears fruit with seed in it according to their various kinds." Genesis ch.1 v11

In the beginning God created all kinds of vegetation, before he created animals and man so they could eat fresh produce. Trees produced fruit with seed in it, according to their various kinds. Each tree God made in its special way. There are thousands of trees all different with their kinds across the earth. He didn't make a oak tree into a maple tree, each tree had a unique kind of growing. God selected various kinds of trees.

Nobody could assume that all the trees came from one stock. It is ludicrous and laughable and nobody is that silly. We have all kinds of seed, some good, some bad, we are not sure of what it is like - it's all the same sort of seed. God grows the seed and makes the plants grow, sometimes a tree or a plant. Look at the seeds; we can't grow any of them with all our specialist equipment. It needs soil, water and sunlight from God.

- - - - - - -

Cain worked the soil. In the course of time Cain brought some of the fruits of the soil as an offering to the Lord. Genesis ch.4 v2-3

After man and woman sinned against God, Cain and Abel were removed out of the Garden of Eden and worked the ground. Cain produced fruit and Abel produced sheep. God looked at Abel and was pleased with what he had done. The contrast is not between an offering of plant life and an offering of animal life, but between a careless, meaningless offering and a choice, generous offering. God looked for a motivation and attitude of heart (it is the same as the thought when we covered 'Attacked').

So Cain killed Abel out in the fields (see Genesis ch.4 v8), where Adam and Eve were not even there, but God knows what Cain has done. This is the first time violence has been done and it is the curse of doing wrong things.

- - - - - - -

Go up through the Negev and on into the hill country. See what the land is like and whether the people who live there are strong or weak, few or many. What kind of land do they live in? is it good or bad? What kinds of towns do they live in? Are they unwalled or fortified? How is the soil? Is it fertile or poor? Are there trees on it or not? Do you best to bring back some of the fruit of the land. Numbers ch.13 v17-20

When the Israelites moved out of slavery in Egypt, they were looking for the Promised Land. They moved up until they reached the Desert of Zin, a place called Kadesh-barnea. Israel went up to Mount Hor, the northern extremity of the Canaanites.

They were looking for the soil of the land, is it fertile? Are there any trees on it? We know that the land of Canaan it is the best fertile soil that they could use, it is the Fertile Crescent. The land forming between Egypt and passing through Canaan upwards by Syria; but they didn't know even that.

When they arrived they planted seed and harvested it. Before the next seed will be sown they will be collecting more produce from the land (see Leviticus ch.26 v5, v10).

They sowed fields and planted vineyards that yielded a fruitful harvest. Psalm ch.107 v37

If they obeyed the word of the Lord, the harvest would be great. But if they didn't, the rain would cease to fall, the soil will be hard to break up, the locusts would eat their crops and the harvest would be poor.

The Israelites would endure a famine by neglecting the word of the Lord and God's instructions for looking after their Promised Land.

- - - - - - -

Does a farmer always plow and never sow? Is he forever cultivating the soil and never planting? Does he not finally plant his seeds—black cumin, cumin, wheat, barley, and emmer wheat—each in its proper way, and each in its proper place? The farmer knows just what to do, for God has given him understanding. A heavy sledge is never used to thresh black cumin; rather, it is beaten with a light stick. A threshing wheel is never rolled on cumin; instead, it is beaten lightly with a flail. Grain for bread is easily crushed, so he doesn't keep on pounding it. He threshes it under the wheels of a cart, but he doesn't pulverize it. Isaiah ch.28 v24-28 (NLT)

All this comes from the Lord Almighty, wonderful in counsel and magnificence in wisdom. Isaiah ch.28 v29

The farmer knows what to do for his crops, for he is taught by God who has given him understanding. It is not true to say that man spent a long time clearing the bushes and trees, he had only a small part of the land to work with, gradually over the years he added more.

When the Lord cursed the ground and Adam and Eve were left to manage as best they can. But trees and plants grew into fearsome shapes, sticking out all over the place, forests and bracken were there, weeds grew up and it was hard and a struggle for man to manage. God said that you will have 'painful toil' to master the work to be done (see Genesis ch.3 v17).

God said, It will produce thorns and thistles for you, and you will eat the plants of the field. By the sweat of your brow you will eat the food. Genesis ch.3 v18-19

God said if you follow me and serve me, I will make it easier for you.

- - - - - - -

Jesus said, "A farmer went out to sow his seed." Matthew ch.13 v3

The parable of The Sower means that a farmer sows his seed:

Along the path the birds came and ate the seed.

Rocky places where there's not much soil.

Thorns which grew up and choked the seed.

Good soil which grew up to have a harvest.

The idea is that the sower scatters the seed by hand movement to sow it on the ground. Some will fall among not so good places but others will lead to the harvest. This is what you have to do, sow the seed into the good, rich land to produce a wonderful harvest.

Whoever has will be given more, and he will have an abundance. Whoever does not have, even what he has will be taken from him. Matthew ch.13 v12

Do you know what that means? Think about the treasure in heaven, so what do you do? Sow the seed from God and reap the harvest in heaven (Matthew ch.6 v19-21).

Stones

Stones a detached piece of rock, usually small.

They used brick instead of stone, and bitumen for mortar. Genesis ch.11 v3

After the flood came, the people used brick instead of stone. Why did they use brick? In the past they used stone and it was hard and the weather didn't effect it at all.

Most of the ancient people were dead with the flood and they took with them the skills they prepared to fit stones. So close together that we couldn't see through it and no mortar. The stones were tightly formed together and they were not in rows. With earthquakes the stones would hold tightly together. They were expert in stone masonry and had machines that could cut the stones flat and smooth.

The people had cutting machines but they were destroyed by the waters that covered all of the mountains (see Genesis ch.7 v23). The Nephilim were on the earth in those early days (see Genesis ch.6 v4) and that's why they moved great stones weighing hundreds of pounds in weight.

Nephilim: were people of great size and strength. Later, when the Israelites went into the Promised Land to investigate they found the Nephilim there (see Numbers ch.13 v33), 'We seemed to be like grasshoppers in their sight'. The men of Anek were men of great stature; their physical size brought fear to the people but Caleb was to drive them from their city (see Joshua ch.15 v14; Judges ch.1 v9-10).

- - - - - - -

But a heavy stone covered the mouth of the well. It was the custom there to wait for all the flocks to arrive before removing the stone and watering the animals. Afterward the stone would be placed back over the mouth of the well. Genesis ch.29 v2–3 (NLT)

Well: an artificial shaft sunk deep to reach the underground water.

The pulley wheel was made a wood and was probably set in some sort of wooden cross-beams. A stone covered up the mouth of the well, to avoid creatures entering it. If it is dark and the well was not covered up people and animals could fall into it.

The well would be a good size so the stone must have been heavy. It would take several men to move it away. This is why all the flocks would come to be watered and men would be standing near by, to heave the stone out of the way. In the arid parts, water may have become as precious as gold. Wells could remain the subjects of fierce disputes and even strife (see Genesis ch.13 v6-9).

- - - - - - -

Jacob set up a stone pillar at the same place where God had talked with him, and he poured a drink offering on it; he also poured oil on it. Genesis ch.35 v14

Rectangular stone pillars were used in large houses for carrying upper storeys. Such stones were commonly used. The wood would not have been commonly used because of the weight and the size of the building.

Stones set up and used throughout the ancient world would often been associated with a shrine or temple. Important events were used and oil poured out on top, marking them out from other stones. In the Canaanite religion, the pillar had so far become identified with the deity. It was therefore forbidden to be used by the Israelites who were told to destroy such sites, like 'their sacred stones to pieces' (see Exodus ch.23 v24).

It was therefore common to erect large stones and place oil of top, which marked out which stones were to be removed by the Israelites. The oil would not be removed by the rain.

- - - - - - -

Aaron did just as the Lord had commanded Moses. He eventually placed it in the Ark of the Covenant—in front of the stone tablets inscribed with the terms of the covenant. Exodus ch.16 v34 (NLT)

God inscribed with his finger the two stone tablets with his covenant which was to be kept in the ark that had made (see Deuteronomy ch.9 v10, ch.10 v5). The two tablets were smashed or broken up when Moses went down the Mount Sinai. When the people had made a golden calf because Moses didn't appear; he was there for 40 days and nights (see Deuteronomy ch.9 v17).

God told Moses to make new tablets like the first ones, to be chiselled out of stone, God wrote on them the Ten Commandments as he did the first ones (see Deuteronomy ch.10 v4). This was the most important role that God gave to Moses. He stored it in the ark to be carried when the people moved around and it was there for over many years.

- - - - - - -

Then Moses cried out to the Lord, "What am I to do with these people? They are almost ready to stone me." Exodus ch.17 v4

Stoning was the usual Israelite form of execution (see Exodus ch.19 v13). The prosecution witness had to cast the first stone (see Deuteronomy ch.13 v9-10). After if the victim still lived, the others had to stone him to death. The body was suspended on a tree until sunset (see Deuteronomy ch.21 v23). To warn others that if a man is guilty of a capital offence it was a disgrace for the Israelites.

Stoning was the situation of the victim in the middle of a circle. The stones were heavy and the individual was caught by all the stones falling on him and there was many large stones around (see Joshua ch.7 v24-26). The purpose of stoning was all the people together would have a hand in it to remove the victim from his evil practice.

In the New Testament the Apostle Paul lay down in the ground and protected his face with his hands, but still it was a circle so that Paul couldn't get away (see Acts ch.14 v19-20). But he was still outside the city walls but the crowd left him there to die. They didn't realise that he was still alive.

Any Israelite or any alien living in Israel who gives any of his children to Molech must be put to death. The people of the community are to stone him. Leviticus ch.20 v1-2

The reason is that Molech was a god worshipped by the Ammonites was associated with the sacrifice of children in the fire. The exile seems to have put an end to this worship, but it lingered on into north Africa.

The Israelites are to stone the person to death. Because it was an evil practice where children are subject to be burnt alive (see Jeremiah ch.32 v35).

- - - - - - -

Reaching into his bag and taking out a stone, he slung it and struck the Philistine on the forehead. The stone sank deep into his forehead, and he fell face down on the ground. 1 Samuel ch.17 v49

David a young man of Israel and the giant Goliath the Philistine, met when the two armies had met in Secoh in Judah (see 1 Samuel ch.17 v1). Goliath was over nine feet tall, a bronze helmet on his head and he was covered with a coat of bronze scale armour weighing 5,000 shekels. On his legs he had bronze greaves, and a bronze javelin was slung on his back. His spear shaft weighed in at 600 shekels and his shield bearer went ahead of him.

David didn't wear armour at all and he didn't have a sword, but he had a sling and only 5 stones (see 1 Samuel ch.17 v40).

Slings were usually used by shepherds to ward off wild beasts and to prevent the animals from straying. The Egyptians, the Assyrians and Babylonians used it for war. The tribe of Benjamin were able to use slings left and right handed (see 1 Chronicles ch.12 v2) and they would not miss (see Judges ch.20 v16).

The use of a sling was David's choice and the first stone sank deep into Goliath's forehead. David was not concerned about his weapons nor his armour but he knew that Goliath must see him. Goliath's face was unprotected, but the young boy new he couldn't miss. The lion and the bear rounded on him and he was marked out as bait for them. They wanted to take a sheep away but David the shepherd was in the way (see 1 Samuel ch.17 v34-36).

- - - - - - -

At the king's command they removed from the quarry large block of quality stone to provide a foundation of dressed stone for the temple. The craftsmen of Solomon and Hiram and the men of Gebal cut and prepared the timber and stone for the building. 1 Kings ch.5 v17-18

The men used from the quarry a 'large block of quality stone' to make the temple foundation done correctly. Stones were a convenient form of building work to get the foundations. All the building was on top of the foundations, so they have to be of stone. The craftsmen cut and prepared timber and stone in the quarry and not at the temple in Jerusalem. The reason for it was quiet, the work of chiselling out was done in the quarry.

The men at the quarry understood about the 'quality stone' and they had reason to look at the stone and find only particles and not find cuts and other rocks in the middle. They were skilled and knowledgeable able to grasp what stone would have been used. They had chisels and levels to separate the 'dressed stone' for the foundations.

Resentment among the people towards this form of slave labour eventually led to the division of king Solomon kingdom, immediately after his death (see 1 Kings ch.5 v13).

- - - - - - -

You will overthrow every fortified city and every major town. You will cut down every good tree, stop-up all the good springs, and ruin every good field with stones. 2 Kings ch.3 v19

In the time of the prophet Elisha, Moab revolts. The king of Moab didn't want to supply the king of Israel with 100,000 lambs and the wool of 100,000 rams. He decided to rebel when king Ahab died because there was animosity between the pair of them as kings.

When the king of Moab saw that the battle had gone against him, he took 700 swordsmen to break through to the king of Edom but they failed. Then he offered his firstborn son as a crown prince and offered him as a sacrifice on the city wall as a burnt offering to the Moabite god Chemosh. It was a dreadful thing to carry out (see 2 Kings ch.3 v27). War and the reaction to it, makes grown men take wilful action and violence against poor innocent people, that in peacetime they would even shudder to do it.

War is started by lot of reasons but the end result is that you will ruin every good field with stones. Moab had lot of sheep but the stones would affect them badly, the sheep could not enter the 'good fields'. Eventually Moab and Israel would hate and spite each other. Because they were neighbours.

Sword

Sword a weapon with a long blade, sharp on one of both edges for cutting or thrusting.

The sword is the most frequently mentioned weapon in the Bible. The straight blade was made of iron or a blacksmith sharpened the sword (see 1 Samuel ch.13 v19). It hung on the left hand side from a girdle and was ususally in a sheath (see 2 Samuel ch.20 v8). But they didn't have guns, tanks, warships or planes, they came much later. In the early days one would fight another, but now with more weapons we can use them to annihilate whole cities and buildings.

After he drove the man out, he placed on the east side of the Garden of Eden cherubim and a flaming sword flashing back and forth to guard the way to the tree of life. Genesis ch.3 v24

The first mention of a sword is from God, to separate man from coming to take the tree of life. If he had done so, God would be separated himself because of his holy and righteous manner. Man could not have gone to heaven but he would be separated from God for ever. This was why God had a cherubim and a flaming sword to keep mankind off. It was not an angel, it was a cherubim a special one to keep the two of them away.

Later, two gold cherubim would be there on the front of the ark of the testimony, they are to face each other. There God will met with you and give you all my commands (see Exodus ch.25 v19-22). This was a holy place where God would meet Moses. The cherubim would be there to guard God when he moves around (see Psalm ch.99 v1).

- - - - - - -

You will live by the sword and you will serve your brother. But when you grow restless, you will throw his yoke from off your neck. Genesis ch.27 v40

Jacob had received Isaac's blessing while Isaac was old and his eyes were weak (see Genesis ch.27 v1). Jacob deceived Isaac by putting on Esau's clothes and covering himself with goatskins, Jacob has not a hairy man like Esau (see Genesis ch.27 v15-16). Esau was furious against Jacob and wanted to kill him (see Genesis ch.27 v42-44). Esau was very handy with a sword because he was a hunter and would kill his game. But Jacob ran away, he fled to Laban, Rebekah's brother. It is a pity, since Rebekah (his mother) told Jacob what he should do and the two brother's fought over the blessing. Which was really important.

- - - - - - -

Now let us take a three-day journey into the desert to offer sacrifices to the Lord our God, or he may strike us with plagues or with the sword. Exodus ch.5 v3

The Israelites were slaves in Egypt under the Pharaoh, but they wanted to move out and throw off slavery once and for all. They were badly ill-treated because they were numerous and might take sides against Egypt (see Exodus ch.1 v9-10).

Moses and Aaron went to see Pharaoh and explained that they wanted to go into the desert to sacrifice to God. Pharaoh didn't want them to go, all of his slaves for a three-day journey, he might lose some of them but he wanted to keep the slaves busy working on his bricks and fields (see Exodus ch.5 v5).

God sent the plagues upon Egypt to force them to let the Israelites go. It might take more than a year, as each plague compelled the Israelites to leave Egypt, but the last plague affected everybody, most of the Egyptians died at midnight, the Lord struck down the firstborn in the land, even the prisoner who was in the dungeon (see Exodus ch.12 v31-36). The Lord was with the Israelites and didn't want to hurt them with a sword with the last plague.

- - - - - - -

They will stumble over one another as though fleeing from the sword, even though no-one is pursuing them. So you will not be able to stand before your enemies. You will perish among the nations; the land of your enemies will devour you. Leviticus ch.26 v37–38

Once they had been freed from slavery, God led them through the Wilderness of Paran, to go to Mount Sinai where God met with them there. He spent a long time with Moses outlining the work that he wanted them to do before they reached the Promised Land. He explained that there were two kinds of path: obedience and disobedience. He wanted the people there to follow him and obey his instructions. If they didn't do that, the enemies would overtake them.

It was not the Israelites, nor the people where they were going. God himself was going to pursue them with the sword and wipe them out and that is what happened. Once in the Promised Land with all the good things that they could enjoy, they disregarded and forgot about God. Over the centuries they ignored and separated themselves from God. He sent prophets to warn them but they ill-treated them (see Acts ch.7 v51-53).

Violence

Violence is intensely forcible, impetuous and unrestrained in furious action.

Now God saw that the earth had become corrupt and was filled with violence. God observed all this corruption in the world, for everyone on earth was corrupt. So God said to Noah, "I have decided to destroy all living creatures, for they have filled the earth with violence. Yes, I will wipe them all out along with the earth!" Genesis ch.6 v11-13 (NLT)

God saw all men were corrupt and the land was filled with violence. He said I have decided to wipe all men out, but Noah his family I will save and the birds and animals too. God was grieved that he had made men on the earth, rather than giving God the glory, they were filled with violence.

It was a terrible thing to have to come to the Lord with bitterness, evil and violence and he would cast us out of heaven. God doesn't change, if the earth was like that, God will wipe it out not by flood, but by fire (see 2 Peter ch.3 v6-7). Only Noah was saved but all the people 'were corrupt and filled with violence', only 8 people were saved by the flood and the waters swept across the mountains and man, God's animals and birds died (see Genesis ch.7 v19-23).

God is patient and kind but he would do the same thing if the violence would still be there among the people who are currently living today. It is the same reason that the evil, violence and swords would increase day by day. We notice that and are sickened by what we read in the papers, the social media and the television.

- - - - - - -

Simeon and Levi are brothers - their swords are weapons of violence. Genesis ch.49 v5

Simeon and Levi took it out with the Shechemities because Shechem had raped Dinah the daughter of Jacob (see Genesis ch.34). The two of them seized everything: (We can see that with 'Weapons')

They killed every male.

They looted the city.

They took their flocks, herds and donkeys away.

They carried off all of their wealth.

They took their women and children.

They replied to Jacob, 'He has treated our sister like a prostitute' and that never should have been done (see Genesis ch.34 v31).

Jacob said, "Cursed by their anger, so fierce, and their fury, so cruel!" Genesis ch.49 v7

Jacob said, 'Simeon and Levi they shared the traits of violence, anger and cruelty'. That is what he remarked when he blessed his sons at the end of his life. He didn't say anything to encourage them, he remembered and thought about it with the Shechemites. But he didn't correct his sons and moved away with his family to Bethel.

This is often called the 'Blessing of Jacob' and it is the longest poem in the book of Genesis. This was a reflection and a warning of what they could be doing in the Promised Land. The children of the pair of them were there with all the Israelites but they had the forewarning of what might happen.

- - - - - - - -

The Lord examines the righteous, but the wicked and those who love violence his soul hates. Psalm ch.11 v5

God hates violence where ever he finds it. Violence with the passion that comes from it, it is excessively cruel and unrestrained. This is why the person who has it is totally destructive and savage.

When God flooded the earth, he said that the people were full of violence. There was a lot of things they were doing, but violence was the key to all of it. It was the intensity and ferocity of what they were doing and even male and female were going round arguing and fighting with each other.

Do not hand me over to the desire of my foes, for false witnesses rise up against me, breathing out violence. Psalm ch.27 v12

'Breathing out violence' these witnesses in their hearts and they were trying to get king David out, whenever they thought possible. Their was no room for possible negotiations they were determined to get him removed. False witnesses, lying cheats, making-it-up as they went along. They ganged up together as one body to cheat him out of his kingdom.

King David confidently expresses his faith to deliver him from his enemies. He was thinking about God, though an army would come against his people and God even has a plan. Even the king had serious problem keeping his counsellors in check, but his security in the Lord would keep his enemies at bay.

Confuse the wicked, O Lord, confound their speech, for I see violence and strife in the city. Psalm ch.55 v9

'Confound their speech'; confuse their intentions. For king David that in his place in Jerusalem, there were people going round, in and down their paths, even talking about them. 'Malice and abuse are within the city'. There was violence in the streets, down on the streets going though the city. Men talked to men, but king David could see and understand them. He said, 'Do not ignore my plea' (see Psalm ch.55 v1).

No, in your heart you devise injustice, and your hands mete violence on the earth. Psalm ch.58 v2

'There venom is like the venom of a snake', they didn't understand that the violence was sufficiently bad, that they 'would not listen to a snake charmer' (see Psalm ch.58 v4-5). Their hands would take their hostility to its aggression, to take it out on the people on the earth. 'You devise injustice', says king David. The courts should be a place of mutual consultation, it is why we have judges that know the law (see Leviticus ch.19 v15).

When looking through king David's time, there was indeed peace, David took it out on the nations around Israel, he was marked out for good and people were happy (see 1 Samuel ch.18 v5-7). But the reason is different, people in Jerusalem want change and violence is everywhere, but David looks to God and worships him.

Warrior

Warrior a skilled fighting man or a distinguished fighter.

Cush was the father of Nimrod, who grew up to be a mighty warrior on the earth. Genesis ch.10 v8

Nimrod was the first warrior on the earth. He was a descendant of Ham who was the son of Noah. He was the firstborn Cush, who was the father of Nimrod.

Nimrod was a mighty hunter before the Lord, but he was a warrior, a skilled fighter for God. This was most unusual, because most of the people in the first book of the Bible and not associated with a 'warrior'. He was a mighty warrior on the earth, meaning he was going into battle a lot of times and had a good reason to do it. Probably to try to stop the violence all around.

- - - - - - -

Jephthah the Gilead was a mighty warrior. Judges ch.11 v1

Gideon defeated the Midianites because the power of the Midian was so oppressive the Israelites prepared shelters for themselves in nearby rocks (see Judges ch.6 v1-2, v11). Jephthah his father was Gilead and his mother was a prostitute. Gilead's wife also bore him sons and when they were grown up they drove Jephthah away. You are not going to receive any inheritance from my father, said his sons (see Judges ch.11 v1-2), 'Because you are a son of another woman'.

Some time later the Ammonites made war on Israel, the elders of Gilead turned to Jephthah who was a warrior, 'Be our commander' (see Judges ch.11 v5-6). He agreed because he wanted to be head and had control over them (see Judges ch.11 v9).

Then the Spirit of the Lord came upon Jephthah, he devastated 20 towns, thus Israel subdued Ammon (see Judges ch.11 v29, v33). He was a mighty warrior to do the Lord's work, to save Israel from Ammon.

- - - - - - -

For all Israel knows what a mighty warrior your father (David) is and how courageous his men are. 2 Samuel ch.17 v10 (NLT)

I have bestowed strength on a warrior; I have exalted a young man from among the people. I have found David my servant; with my sacred oil I have anointed him. My hand will sustain him; surely my arm will strengthen him. Psalm ch.89 v19–21

There are many battles in the records where king David had defeated many kingdoms (see 1 Chronicles ch.17 v7-8). David was a known warrior he had conquered many kingdoms alongside of Israel. He picked courageous men who would support him (see 2 Samuel ch.23 v8-39). David looked to God who strengthened him, together they fought the nations around them. God was pleased that David mustered his battles to fight and get the Israel to do what the Lord had intended to do for Abraham's covenant (see Genesis ch.15 v18-21).

The arrangement of the temple of God should remain with his son, Solomon, who would build and construct it. King Solomon was a man of peace not a warrior.

- - - - - - -

There was also Benaiah son of Jehoiada, a valiant warrior from Kabzeel. He did many heroic deeds, which included killing two champions of Moab. Another time, on a snowy day, he chased a lion down into a pit and killed it. Once, armed only with a club, he killed a great Egyptian warrior who was armed with a spear. Benaiah wrenched the spear from the Egyptian's hand and killed him with it. 2 Samuel ch.23 v20–21 (NLT)

Benaiah was a warrior and he was in charge of David's bodyguard (see 2 Samuel ch.23 v23). King David had included him to let Solomon be king (see 1 Kings ch.1 v44). Later, after king David had died, Benaiah was still there protecting king Solomon (see 1 Kings ch.2 v25). He struck Joab the commander of Israel's army and killed him and Joab was buried in his own land in the desert (see 1 Kings v34). King Solomon put Benaiah over the army instead of Joab (see 1 Kings ch.2 v35).

Benaiah was a warrior and he helped David as his bodyguard and Solomon as his commander of the army.

- - - - - - -

The king of Aram had great admiration for Naaman, the commander of his army, because through him the Lord had given Aram great victories. But though Naaman was a mighty warrior, he suffered from leprosy. 2 Kings ch.5 v1 (NLT)

Naaman was a commander of Aram's army but he had leprosy, which means he would be separate and all of his clothes would be washed continuously. He was a mighty warrior, but he was cured by the prophet Elisha (see 2 Kings ch.5). Naaman was sent to Israel because of a young slave girl from Israel who served Naaman's wife.

The leprosy was incurable and if you had it, you would eventually die because your fingers and toes would go black and drop off. Leprosy covered a number of conditions in the Bible, but in the past the treatment of leprosy was bad and messy. In Israel the person had to go out of the town or city wall and stay there until he died (see Leviticus ch.13 v45-46).

- - - - - - -

Zadok, a brave young warrior, with 22 officers from his family. 1 Chronicles ch.12 v28

He was a priest at king David's court along with Abiathar (see 2 Samuel ch.8 v17), he had charge of the ark of God (see 2 Samuel ch.15 v24-29). He supported the anointing of Solomon rather than Adonijah (see 1 Kings ch.1 v7-8).

But he was 'a brave young warrior' armed for battle who came to David at Hebron who volunteered to serve in the ranks. To let David be king over all Israel (see 1 Chronicles ch.12 v38). Even Zadok was a priest but he still was a 'brave young warrior' who fought with David. He was a capable man who had officers from his family.

- - - - - - -

Zicri, an Ephraimite warrior, killed Maasaiah the king's son. 2 Chronicles ch.28 v7

An Ephraimite warrior in the reign of king Pekah who reigned from 734-735 BC. He was noted by his brave action to kill the king's son. There was a great battle against the Arameans who brought many of the Israelites to Damascus. The prophet of the Lord named Obed went out to meet them there when they went back to Samaria. They took a large amount of Aram slaves back to Israel.

No king is saved by the size of his army; no warrior escapes by his great strength. Psalm ch.33 v16

It is important that a warrior must conserve his great strength in battle and not come across as violent and impetuous. This is what the Lord means, no king shall escape with the number of men he has in his army. It is the Lord who decides what the action or cause must be. Whether a large or small army that one has arranged by might or action.

No warrior can survive without the Lord's help. God's assistance will decide the battle whether it is little or large. It is the total strength of men with soldiers or tanks or planes that means so much today. It is so easy to remember that God hold us in his hand and he decides the outcome, whether good or bad.

Weapons

Weapons are any instrument of offence and defence.

Their swords are weapons of violence. Genesis ch.49 v5

When Jacob gave his sons their blessing, he said to Simeon and Levi their swords will go before them. Their weapons would be swords and not peace or joy. But they ransacked the place where the Hivite lives. Each one had his sword by his side and they cut down many who are not well enough to fight. They were circumcised then the swelling should be reduced each day, it makes it difficult to think and plan.

The two of them their swords were weapons of brutality and passion. They didn't leave anyone alive, they kept on going through the city, hacking away with ferocity and meanness. No building was safe to be in.

- - - - - - -

"We will go up and fight, as the Lord our God commanded us." So every one of you put on his weapons, thinking it was easy to go up into the hill country. Deuteronomy ch.1 v41

When the exploration to go into the Promised Land was over. The people rebelled and didn't want to go. 'You grumbled in your tents' (see Deuteronomy ch.1 v27). In spite of this you did not trust in the Lord (see Deuteronomy ch.1 v32). So Moses told you but you would not listen, the Amorites who lived in those hills chased you all the way back to Hormah (see Deuteronomy ch.1 v44).

Weapons are only as good as God intends what you have to do.

- - - - - - - -

So 600 men from the tribe of Dan, armed with weapons of war, set out from Zorah and Eshtaol. Judges ch.18 v11 (NLT)

The men of Dan thought they could do much better in the north because they had not come into their inheritance (see Judges ch.18 v1). They equipped 600 men with weapons of war and journeyed to a place near Sidon. The people there did not have any contact with the rest of the inhabitants, they were alone and had no relationship with anyone else. The tribes of Dan wiped them out and rebuilt the city (see Judges ch.18 v28).

Each territory had a plan provided by God (see Numbers ch.34), but Dan had a problem with their inheritance. So they decided to get it and wiped out the city near Sidon. In these days Israel had no king to stop them. It is going against what God had decided.

Still others to make weapons of war and equipment for his chariots. 1 Samuel ch.8 v12

In the time of Samuel the people wanted a king, but they displeased the prophet who complained to the Lord. God said, 'It is me who they are rejecting as their king' (see 1 Samuel ch.8 v7), 'give the people what they want, but tell them the price of the king they selected' (see 2 Samuel ch.8 v9).

The king wanted to make weapons of war to fight against the nations around them. It is the only thing that a king has, to lead his men into battle.

- - - - - - -

Oh, how the mighty heroes have fallen! Stripped of their weapons, they lie dead. 2 Samuel ch.1 v27 (NLT)

Saul was made king over Israel. The Philistines who were close to the Mediterranean Sea fought against them and overcame them. King Saul and his boys were dead. It doesn't matter how many weapons you have got, there will be always someone who has more weapons than you. They failed to get help from God who is in control. King Saul went to a medium (1

Samuel ch.28) and chased David to kill him and eliminate him from being king after Saul. But he failed in his task.

- - - - - - -

You have chariots and horses, a fortified city and weapons. 2 Kings ch.10 v2

Much later, while king Ahab who had 70 sons (see 2 Kings ch.10 v1). So Jehu wrote letters to the elders and guardians of king Ahab's children then fight for your master throne. But they were terrified and wouldn't do it, to put one of king Ahab's children on his throne (see 2 Kings ch.10 v4).

They had chariots, they had weapons and a fortified city. Jehu wrote a second letter and told them to kill all of the boys (see 2 Kings ch.10 v7). The word of the Lord had spoken to king Ahab by the prophet Elijah then Jehu killed all of Ahab's family, he destroyed them (see 2 Kings ch.10 v17).

- - - - - - -

There he broke the flashing arrows, the shields and the swords, the weapons of war. Psalm ch.76 v3

We don't know who wrote this Psalm, it probably came from after the Lord's destruction of Sennacharib, king of Assyria's army when it threatened Jerusalem (see 2 Kings ch.19 v35). The army was very good and they had destroyed all of the other kings, taken away their gods, decimated there lands (see 2 Kings ch.19 v11-13).

They were exceptionally cruel, taking all the solders away and leaving the land destitute. They chained the people together with chains and going barefoot without any clothes (see Isaiah ch.28 v2). They were exceeding good with weapons of war.

The time will surely come when you will be taken away with hooks the last of you with fish-hooks. You will each go straight out through breaks in the wall you will be cast out towards Hermon, declares the Sovereign Lord Amos ch.4 v2-3

It will be barbaric and sadistic, that Israel would go through the wall, it was the last time they saw the damage of the place where they belonged and they would be a long way off up north from the Promised Land.

- - - - - - -

Wisdom is better than weapons of war; but one sinner destroys much good. Ecclesiastes ch.9 v18

King Solomon reflected foolishness always inclines a man to do wrong and marks him out as a fool. Idleness bring deterioration, if you want to enjoy the good things of life you must have the money to buy them. The wise man will learn to control his thoughts and his speech and to keep out of trouble.

Better to let 'weapons of war' cease; wisdom is the key to finding the path to follow.

Wounding

Wounding is any open injury caused by cutting or striking.

All day long the battle raged, and the king was propped up in his chariot facing the Arameans. The blood from his wound ran on to the floor of the chariot, and that evening he died. 1 Kings ch.22 v35

King Ahab of Israel and king Jehoshaphat of Judah would come together because there was no war between them, together they formed an alliance and attacked Ramoth Gilead. Because Ramoth Gilead belong to the king of Aram and we let the Arameans retake, and control it (see 1 Kings ch.22 v3).

King Ahab went into battle in disguise he wasn't wearing his royal outfit, but someone drew his bow at random and struck him between the sections of his armour (see 1 Kings ch.22 v34). He died as the sun was setting. The prophet Micaiah reminded him that he was going to die in the battle, but he himself thought, if I don't wear royal robes who can find me or wound me?

- - - - - - -

Telling lies about others is as harmful as hitting them with an ax, wounding them with a sword, or shooting them with a sharp arrow. Proverbs ch.25 v18 (NLT)

Lies against the Israelite neighbour is worse than being hit with an axe, sword or an arrow. Why? Because king Solomon understood the whole situation: men didn't trust their neighbours and the whole town came to ruin. We club together, that is why we have towns and cities. We need each other to help us. If you are on your own there is no one around, you will get lonely, desperate and afraid.

Lies separate friends.

- - - - - - -

"Therefore, I will wound you! I will bring you to ruin for all your sins. You will eat but never have enough. Your hunger pangs and emptiness will remain. And though you try to save your money, it will come to nothing in the end. You will save a little, but I will give it to those who conquer you. You will plant crops but not harvest them. You will press your olives but not get enough oil to anoint yourselves. You will trample the grapes but get no juice to make your wine. Micah ch.6 v13-15 (NLT)

God's message for Israel it is a reference back to when they were going into the Promised Land (see Deuteronomy ch.28). You will sow, but will be hungry and God will pass it on to the invaders. Time and time again, the law of Moses wasn't read by those who should read it every day. The book of the law was dusty and covered with cobwebs in the temple (see 2 Kings ch.22 v8-11).

They attacked and killed the prophets who asked them to return back to the Lord. The prophets pleaded with them and entreated the persons, but no, it was not enough. God could not have done more and the Assyrian empire took the Israelites away.

- - - - - - -

They dress the wound of my people as though it was not serious. "Peace, peace," they say, "when there is no peace." Jeremiah ch.6 v14 and ch.8 v11

Jerusalem is still under siege by the Babylonian empire, they were surrounded, all the gates will be shut and no-one will go in or out. People look over at the walls and see the soldiers going up and down, sharpening their weapons and seeing what they were doing. King Zedekiah was on the throne and he was the prophet Jeremiah was referring to (see Jeremiah ch.34 v2-3).

God knew that the city would fall (see 2 Kings ch.25 v3-4). There was 'no real peace' and the city would be taken. The temple and the walls will be burnt down (see 2 Kings ch.25 v9-10). Jeremiah was there in prison and he would be aware that all the people still in the city would be taken away wounded to captivity.

This is what the Lord says: You wound is incurable, your injury beyond healing. There is no-one to plead your cause, no remedy for your sore, no healing for you. Jeremiah ch.30 v12-13

Egypt supported Judah against the Babylonian threat. But the cause of Pharaoh was weakened and he would not risk being part of an unsupported effort (see Jeremiah ch.37 v5-7).

King Zedekiah rebelled against king Nebuchadnezzar and the retaliation came swiftly (see 2 Kings ch.24 v20). Judah was all alone to face the mighty army of the Chaldeans. This time the Babylonian reprisal was hard and without pity. The cities of Judah fell to the Babylonians and the tribe of Judah was taken way for 70 years. What was left was the poor, the wounded, looking after the fields (see Daniel ch.9 v2).

- - - - - - -

If someone asks him, "What are the wounds on your body?" He will answer, "The wounds I was given at the house of my friends." Zechariah ch.13 v6

False prophets were still a problem after the exile (see Nehemiah ch.6 v12-14) and therefore will still be a issue when the New Testament was completed (see 2 Thessalonians ch.2 v2-4). Perhaps indicating the feelings and actions when a person states the wrong thing and makes it happen.

The false prophets and teachers will still be around today. We don't beat and harm them for it and let them run their churches as they want.

We are sad and avoid them.

The End Of The Book

We asked, were prehistoric men savages?

Looking at the Scriptures we can say that they were intelligent, sophisticated and knowledgeable. Not hiding in some caves, dressed in rags and without any speech, like stone-age men.

The time-scale is not billions of years old, it was new and recent. It is a fallacy that would be taken up in several books, written by some educated persons and passed onto the children to learn from. The reason is simple, men don't study the Bible, or if they could, they would change their simplistic views.

The Bible was written many years ago and it was the standard Jewish, Christian or Islamic text. It has never been altered or amended. It stands as one of the most significant manuscripts. It should be read and studied more carefully.

We think of Cain, a boy who had Adam and Eve as his parents. He and his sons were experts in metal like bronze and iron (see Genesis ch.4 v22). He founded a city (see Genesis ch.4 v17). We read in the Bible that what they were doing was indeed remarkable. This seems to make the ancient traditions worthless.

Going over the Scriptures seeking what God would have you do.